Contents

MODERN TIMES

LONGMAN

LONGMAN GROUP UK LIMITED
Longman House, Burnt Mill, Harlow,
Essex CM20 2JE, England
and Associated Companies throughout the world.

First published 1969
Second edition 1972
Seventeenth impression 1990

ISBN 0-582-20440-2

Produced by Longman Group (FE) Ltd
Printed in Hong Kong

Acknowledgements

For permission to reproduce photographs we are grateful to the following: Paul
Popper Ltd pages 4, 6, 9 (*below*), 41, 50, 57, 66, 99, 103 (*above* and *below*), 105, 106
(*below*) and 120; Radio Times Hulton Picture Library pages 1, 12 (*above* and *below*),
16 (*left* and *right*), 18, 21, 25 (*above* and *below*), 28 (*left* and *right*), 31, 33 (*above* and
below), 36 (*above* and *below*), 39 (*above* and *below*), 42, 46 (*left* and *right*), 48, 53, 60
(*above* and *below*), 64, 70, 72, 73, 76, 78, 79, 84, 87 (*above* and *below*), 88, 90, 97, 101,
106 (*above*), 111,115, 122, 127 (*below*), 135, 140 and 146; Society for Cultural Relations
with the USSR pages 8 (*above*), 11, 23, 30, 69 (*above* and *below*), 133, 136, 137, 138,
152 (*below*), 157 and 160; United Press International Ltd pages 93, 127 (*above*),
142 (*left* and *right*), 144, 150 (*left* and *right*) and 152 (*above* and *centre*).

We have been unable to trace the copyright holders of a table of the Russian population adapted from *The Decline of Imperial Russia* by Professor R. W. Seton-Watson, and
Russia by Sir Donald MacKenzie Wallace, and would appreciate any information
that would enable us to do so.

Preface

The most important event of the twentieth century was the Russian revolution. In November 1917, Communism ceased to be a theory; it became the means of governing one of the world's largest states. Since 1945, many east European nations, and the mighty China, have turned to Communism; the most serious threats to world peace have arisen from quarrels between the Communist nations and the powers of the non-Communist West.

Modern Russia tries to show how the Communist revolution of 1917 arose out of conditions in the old Tsarist Russia, the theories of Karl Marx and, above all, the drive and determination of Lenin. It goes on to trace the development of a powerful industrial nation under Joseph Stalin and the new problems which the Soviet Union faced during the rule of Khrushchev. The lives of these three men span all the important events in the last century of Russia's history. Each of them, too, played a vital part when the Soviet Union was involved in world affairs: during two world wars, the Cold War and the great conflict between Russia and China. To know of these is essential for anyone who wishes to understand the modern world.

All the dates in this book are given in the New Style of the Gregorian or Western Calendar. The Russians used the Old Style from the Julian Calendar until the revolution. The Gregorian Calendar is based on a calculation which shows that the earth takes fractionally less than $365\frac{1}{4}$ days to circle the sun. In addition to the extra day every leap year, one additional day has to be added in some centuries. This had already been introduced in European countries with the result that the Russian calendar was a fortnight behind in 1917. When the Bolsheviks changed to the New Style it meant that the revolution which, according to the Russian calendar of the time, had taken place in October would in future be remembered as the November Revolution.

JOHN ROBOTTOM

Prologue–
'I'll Make Them Pay'

Vladimir Ulyanov was puzzled when a class-mate called him aside to show him a letter she had just received from a friend in St Petersburg, the Russian capital. Soon he was reading the terrible news that his brother, Alexander, had been arrested and charged with plotting to assassinate the Emperor. He rushed home to tell his mother. His father, Count Ulyanov, had died the year before and so she had to make the long journey to St Petersburg alone. No one in Simbirsk would go with her; it was not wise to be friendly with the mother of a political prisoner.

In St Petersburg, she learned that Alexander, a brilliant science student, had joined a group of revolutionaries, the People's Will, which had been set up to assassinate the Emperor and leading figures in the government. He had been arrested after waiting with a group of comrades, armed with home-made bombs, for the Emperor's carriage to pass by. The police had warned Alexander III to stay in the Winter Palace and had turned up themselves to arrest the conspirators.

At the trial, Alexander told the judge, 'My purpose was to aid in the liberation of the unhappy Russian people.' He refused to show any regret, and, asked why he had not tried to escape, said, 'I did not want to escape. I wished to die for my country.' In the early morning of 8 May 1887, Alexander and four others from People's Will were hanged.

Back in Simbirsk, Vladimir read the news. He flung aside the paper and cried out: 'I'll make them pay for this! I swear it.'

Thirty years later, Vladimir Ulyanov was known throughout the world as Lenin, the man who on 8 November 1917 became the head of the first Communist state, the Soviet Union.

Tsar Alexander III and his wife

I

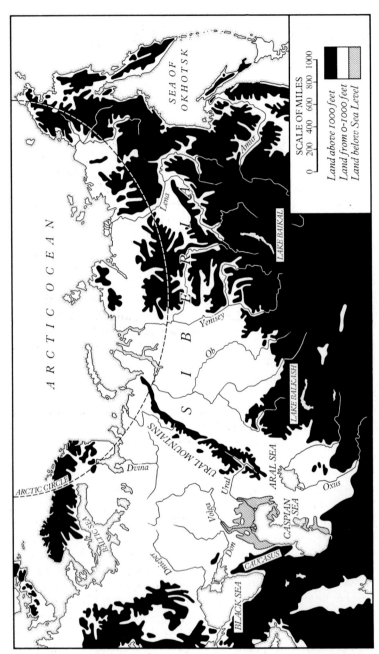

Russia is a low flat land, half enclosed by mountain ranges in the South and East. The Ural mountains separate European Russia from the much larger Siberia. Much of North Russia lies within the Arctic Circle

1 Russia and the Tsars

Vladimir Ulyanov

A month after the execution of Alexander, Vladimir left the high school at Simbirsk, with a gold medal for being the best student 'in ability, development and conduct'. His headmaster recommended him to Kazan University as a model student: 'Neither in nor out of school has a single instance been observed when Ulyanov by word or deed caused dissatisfaction to his teachers or the school authorities.'

But it was only a few weeks before he was in trouble. In December 1887 the students at Kazan presented a petition to the head of the University demanding that they should have the freedom to hold political meetings. In the front row of the demonstrators stood Vladimir. That night he, and forty others, were arrested and expelled from the town. A police officer tried to give him advice: 'Why did you engage in this revolt, young man? Don't you realize you're up against a wall?'

'Yes, a wall, but a rotten one; one kick and it will crumble', replied Vladimir.

What made Vladimir risk his own safety so soon after his own brother had given up his life?

The Tsars

They were both protesting against the system of government under the emperors, or Tsars, of Russia. Since the seventeenth century Russia had been ruled by the Romanov family. Their rule was the perfect example of autocracy—government by one man. There was no parliament or council from which the Tsar had to take advice. There was not even a committee, or cabinet, of ministers. Each of the ministers was the Tsar's personal servant and only the Tsar, and sometimes his wife or a favourite adviser, had a complete picture of the country's problems.

Autocracy had been necessary in the time of the early Tsars,

3

Civil servants in uniform

who had to be ruthless and cruel to prevent power slipping into the hands of powerful landowners. As time went on, and the problems of government became much less simple, the Tsars could only make the autocracy work by employing a huge army of civil servants. Nicholas I once said, 'Russia is governed not by me but by my forty thousand clerks.' The civil servants were graded into fourteen different ranks, from the humblest clerks at the bottom to the governors of the provinces and the ministers at St Petersburg at the top. Each rank carried with it a special uniform and title. Great honours poured on the few who reached the fourth grade, who were made noblemen and given the title of 'Excellency'. Only those with influential friends and relatives ever reached so high.

Many Russians sought after posts in the civil service because they meant a life of ease. At the very least, there was a chance of spending the long cruel winters in a warm office and there were plenty of opportunities for forcing bribes out of the people. Two common Russian proverbs were: 'Any stick will do to beat a thief but only a rouble will help you with an official', and 'The law is like an axle—you can turn it whichever way you please if you give it plenty of grease.'

The officials were given little freedom to make their own decisions. Even minor repairs to a government office required approval from a chain of higher officials which ended at the ministries in St Petersburg. In the reign of Nicholas I, the reports on one case filled 15,000 sheets of paper. The Russians accused the civil service of standing in the way of efforts to develop trade and industry and improve their towns and villages. Men and women were not even allowed to move from one district to another without passports and a pile of documents signed by officials.

The task of the civil service was to keep the autocracy in being and this could not be done if the Russian people were allowed any freedom to govern themselves.

The Okhrana

The job of making sure that the country remained loyal to the Tsar was given to the Minister of the Interior, who kept control by a confusing system of organizations. Russia was divided into fifty provinces, each of which had a governor. Below him were the governors of districts and the commandants of the towns. These men had wide powers and ruled with the help of their own police forces. But apart from these, the Minister of the Interior headed the Secret Police, known in the middle of the

A police round-up in St Petersburg

century as the Third Section and later as the Okhrana. It was the task of these men to seek out persons suspected of opposition to the Tsar. Their powers were very wide. There was no need to prove that a prisoner was plotting against the emperor; any suspect could be exiled to Siberia without any form of trial whatsoever. The Okhrana worked through secret agents who joined suspected organizations, or enrolled as students at a university, to seek out the tiniest breath of criticism. Many of its arrests were quite unjust and thousands of innocent Russians were exiled because the Okhrana was unwilling to admit a mistake. The Okhrana headquarters contained the 'black room' where mail was opened and read before being sent on its way. It had the power to censor all printed books and papers and order the removal of anything of which it disapproved.

The Land

The autocratic Tsars ruled over a country which, by comparison with western Europe, was backward in almost every respect. An English traveller, Mackenzie Wallace, toured the country in the 1860s and wrote a very full account of all he saw. Travel was boring and uncomfortable. There were very few railways because Russia was not the busy industrial nation that England, France and Germany had become at this time. The few trains ran across the unchanging plains at between fifteen and thirty miles an hour carrying passengers who sat surrounded by furs, blankets, pillows and food for a journey that might last for many days.

Most journeys were made by coach, usually a heavy wooden affair rather like a cradle on wheels, with no springs and nothing more than an armful of hay for a seat. Horses were changed at post-stations where passengers rested by stretching out on wooden benches. Very often they were annoyed to find themselves held up by post-station keepers or police chiefs who found some fault with their great bundle of documents. The roads were unsurfaced tracks of great width, due to the efforts of coach drivers to steer to the right or left of the deep ruts made by earlier coaches.

Peasants

In such coaches, Mackenzie Wallace passed along the broad muddy streets which ran through the centre of countless villages. The peasants who lived in them made up more than three-quarters of the Russian population. They lived in roughly-made timber houses whose roofs sloped down from the top of the single room and carried on over the stables and cowsheds. Inside, the only furniture was a rough wooden table, a bench and several stools. The most important object was a large brick stove. From the stove and along one wall ran a wide wooden shelf which served as a bed for the whole family. In the coldest weather peasants often slept on top of the stove itself.

Until 1861 the Russian peasants were serfs, the property of a landowner for whom they had to work three days in the week as well as paying a great number of different fees and rents. The owner controlled the private life of the serf. He chose his wife for him, prevented him from leaving the village or, on the other hand, punished a troublesome serf by forcing him into the army. The landowner had the right to beat his serfs and to sell them.

After 1861 when they were freed, the peasants found that life became harder. Most of them were granted less land than they had farmed as serfs and even this had to be bought from their old masters. As very few peasants had any savings, the government paid the landlords and collected the money by

7

instalments which, in most cases, were to go on until 1932.

Each family had to belong to the *Mir* or village assembly which was responsible to the government for the behaviour of the peasants. The Mir had to issue passports for those who wished to leave the village and was forced to collect heavy taxes to hand over to the government. It was also responsible for re-dividing the village land every few years. The peasants still farmed strips, no more than eight feet wide, in the three huge fields. Farming was extremely primitive. Very few peasants owned more than a crude wooden plough.

As the nineteenth century wore on, the share of land that fell to each peasant became smaller. Russia's population grew from about sixty million to more than a hundred million in the second half of the century, and more people meant smaller farms and less food. Many peasants fell into debt and were forced to borrow from money-lenders at more than twenty per cent interest. Hundreds of thousands left the villages to seek work in city factories, but tens of millions stayed behind to face hardship and hunger. Their difficulties increased as the factories began to mass-produce articles made from leather, cane and wrought iron which previously peasants had made in their own homes and sold.

Landlords

Every few years hunger and misery led to peasant risings. Usually these took the form of attacks on neighbouring land-owners who were rich in land and very often had fields which

Above: a village scene, 1905

Cossacks. The first Cossacks were bands of warriors who had occupied the southern lands of Russia rather like frontiersmen in the American west. In the nineteenth century they were forced to join the Tsar's army, and the mounted Cossack troops became his most feared soldiers

they did not even bother to cultivate. Their houses were damaged and their hay-ricks and stables burned. On such occasions the government sent troops, usually the dreaded Cossacks, cavalry fighters from south Russia, who put down the peasants with great savagery and executed large numbers. Not surprisingly, the landowners feared any change in the system of government which might lead to plans for transferring some of their land to the peasants. They were the firmest supporters of the system of autocracy. Yet most of them did very little to serve their country in any useful way. Mackenzie Wallace described a typical day in the life of a landlord, Ivan Ivanovitch:

'Ivan Ivanovitch gets up about seven o'clock and puts on, with the assistance of his *valet de chambre*, a simple costume consisting chiefly of a faded, plentifully stained dressing gown. Having nothing in particular to do, he sits down at the open window and looks into the yard. . . . Towards nine o'clock tea is announced and he goes into the dining room. . . . As this morning meal consists merely of bread and tea, it does not last long; and all disperse to their several occupations. The head of the house begins the labours of the day by resuming his seat at the open window. When he has smoked some cigarettes he goes out with the intention of visiting the stables and farmyard, but generally before he has crossed the court he finds the heat unbearable, and returns to his former position by the open window. Here he sits tranquilly till the sun has so far moved round that the verandah at the back of the house is completely in the shade, when he has his arm-chair removed thither, and sits there till dinner-time.

'Dinner is the great event of the day. The food is abundant and of good quality, but mushrooms, onions and fat play a rather too important part.

'No sooner has the last dish been removed than a deathlike stillness falls upon the house; it is the time of the afternoon siesta.

'In about two hours the house gradually re-awakes . . . soon a man-servant issues from the kitchen bearing an enormous tea urn which puffs like a little steam engine.

'In the evening it often happens that a little group of peasants come into the court and ask to see the "master". . . .

Peasants eating lunch in the field

Stepping forward a little, and bowing low, one of the group begins in a graceful, half-familiar caressing tone: "Little Father, Ivan Ivanovitch, be gracious; you are our father, and we are your children"—and so on—until at last his patience is exhausted and he says to them in a paternal tone, "Now, enough, enough! You are blockheads—blockheads all round!"

'A regular part of the evening's occupation is the interview with the steward. The work that has just been done, and the programme for the morrow, are always discussed at great length ... till supper is announced and immediately after that meal, all retire for the night.'

There were many critics of the lack of purpose in the lives of the Russian gentry. Most criticism came from the young or the few Russians who had travelled and met the leaders of society in other countries. The Tsars were quite satisfied with a nobility which never made any effort to interfere in the work of the government.

The Priests

The autocracy of the Tsars was strongly upheld by the Russian Orthodox Church. The Church was controlled by a government committee, the Holy Synod, which was headed by one of the Tsar's ministers, the Procurator of the Holy Synod. It was

Inside the Orthodox Church in the Kremlin. The Kremlin was the home of the first Tsars

Leo Tolstoy, author of *War and Peace* and *Anna Karenina* wearing peasant costume–a mark of his belief that the peasant's simple life represented the true greatness of the Russian people

expected to teach respect for the autocracy through its bishops and priests, and in its schools. It provided nearly all Russia's very few schools, where religion and ancient literature were taught to the wealthy. The Tsar and the Church did not want education for the masses who might demand changes in society.

The Bishops watched carefully over the parish priests, even censoring their sermons. Very few parish priests tried to change the ignorance and superstition of the peasants. The peasants despised them for their idleness, and the payments they took for holy days and marriage or burial services. One priest complained to Mackenzie Wallace: 'I can see that the peasants grudge every handful of rye and every egg that they give me. I can hear their sneers as I go away and I know that they have many sayings such as "The priest takes from the living and from the dead."'

The Opposition

The backwardness of Russia, the cruelty of the government and the miserable living conditions of the peasants led to attacks on the autocracy. The earliest criticisms came from the liberals, men and women who compared the state of Russia with conditions in the countries of western Europe, where rapid changes were taking place. Cities were growing into bustling centres of industry. France, Britain and Germany were building a network of railways; new scientific discoveries and inventions were made every year.

These countries, the liberals thought, were thriving because of their more democratic systems of government. In England and France, power had passed from the kings and the land-owning classes into the hands of the middle classes, ruling through parliaments. This had led to many improvements. There was no secret police and judges were not expected to give the verdict the government wanted. Education was encouraged. In Germany one in every eight of the population was in school while the figure for Russia was only one in 376. Life was hard for the poor but there were none of the cruelties still practised in Russia—flogging, for example, or the passport system which prevented people moving about the country and, above all, serfdom were no longer known.

Liberalism was a strong force among educated Russians. Many were from noble families and had grown up deeply ashamed of the idle and purposeless lives led by their friends and relatives. From the great Russian novelists, playwrights and poets of the time they learned to mock the inefficiency and ignorance of civil servants and to hate the cruelty of the secret police. 'God, what sad country Russia is,' said the poet, Pushkin, after reading *Dead Souls*, a tragicomic novel by Gogol. Tolstoy attacked the stupidity and cruelty of the police and law courts in *Resurrection* and he expressed his deep sympathy with the peasants in *Anna Karenina*.

There was a brief time at the beginning of the reign of Alexander II (1858–1881) when the liberals had some success. The Crimean War had exposed Russia's backwardness. The nation had been unable to provide good transportation to southern Russia for her armies who were fighting French and British troops, who had travelled two or three thousand miles to the battlefield. The defeat of Russia was blamed on the inefficient government and led to widespread demands for change. Alexander feared that his empire was on the edge of revolution and tried to weaken the opposition, first by freeing the serfs in 1861 and then by granting some of the reforms called for by the liberals. In 1864 he allowed each district to set up a *zemstvo* or local council with powers to provide roads, schools and medical services. This was a concession to the liberals, not to the masses of the people, for the right to elect zemstvo members was restricted to the wealthy.

In many zemstvos liberals won a majority and set out to use their powers to the fullest. Schools, clinics and doctors' surgeries were opened; some roads and bridges were built. But the zemstvo experiment only sharpened the divisions in Russia. The civil service did everything it could to obstruct the work of the zemstvos. Landowners of the old school resented the zemstvos' attempts to improve the lives of peasants who only a few years before had been their serfs.

Alexander's hopes of winning support for the autocracy were shattered by the continued demands of liberals for more reforms. He began to rely more and more on the civil service, the secret police, the old nobility and the church. Yet his ministers and his police could not crush the new opposition which grew up in the universities.

The Narodniks

One of Alexander's reforms had been to relax police control over university education. For the first time many students heard of socialism, which was a growing movement in the cities of western Europe. Most of the Russian poor were peasants so ignorant that they accepted their way of life because they knew of nothing better. To many young educated Russians it seemed that here was the force which could sweep away the autocracy. If only the tens of millions of peasants could be brought to demand more freedom, more education and more land, they would create a force which no government could stop.

In 1874 the idea was put into practice. Two thousand young men and women put on peasant dress and went into the countryside. This movement 'to the people' (in Russian, *y narod*) earned them the name 'narodniks'. Living with the peasants they helped them by teaching, nursing and giving medical help. At the same time they tried to explain how they hoped the peasants would take part in their campaign for a democratic government. They were disappointed and discovered what one writer meant when he said that the people cared more for potatoes than a constitution.

Although the movement was a failure the government took it seriously. The secret police arrested 1,500 narodniks. The narodniks tried again the following year with the same result; the peasants were not interested, and the police were active.

What then were the narodniks to do? This was the moment when the supporters of terrorism had their chance—for some believed that any form of government was bad and assassination of political leaders was a means of setting the people free. The narodniks set up a special terrorist organization, People's Will, which was to organize attacks on the Tsar and his leading ministers. 'History is terribly slow, it must be pushed forward,' said one of the organizers.

In 1879 they condemned the Tsar to death. There were seven failures before, in March 1881, a bomb was thrown at

Pobedonostsev

Michael Bakunin

the Tsar's carriage, killing one of his guard. Alexander stepped down to look at the bomb thrower who had been seized by the crowd. As he returned to his carriage, a second bomb was thrown. Alexander died an hour later.

Pobedonostsev and the Reaction

The new Tsar, Alexander III, 'mounted the throne as a soldier mounts the breach', determined to crush all opposition. The years which followed 1881 are known as the reaction, the time when the government, and its supporters in the Church and among the landowners, did all they could to undo the advances made under Alexander II.

To organize the reaction Alexander called upon Pobedonostsev, the procurator of the Holy Synod. Pobedonostsev was a firm believer in autocracy. 'Parliamentarianism', he once said, 'is the great lie of our time.' He immediately strengthened the powers of the secret police and made the censorship of books and newspapers even stricter. He then stopped the spread of new schools, which he believed turned the children of the poor into dangerous revolutionaries. The fees for secondary schools were increased so that 'children of coachmen, servants, laundresses, small shop-keepers and the like' would not be able to attend. He clamped down on the universities. Professors were in future to be chosen by the government; students were forbidden to join clubs. Police spies were enrolled as students to see that lectures contained no criticism of the government and to seek out secret organizations among the students.

An even more evil side of the reaction was the persecution of the non-Russian people in the Empire.

The Russian Empire had grown from the tiny state of Muscovy, the area around the city of Moscow. As it expanded the Muscovites, or Great Russians, had conquered people of many different races and religions. Together these 'minority people' made up nearly half the total population of the Empire. In the south they were mostly Asiatic people, many of them Muslims, who had been over-run by the Cossack bands of free Russian fighters. In the west the minority people were the people of Lithuania, the Ukraine and Poland, all of whom

A settlement of Khirghiz people; Muslim nomads who lived near the frontier with China

had been conquered by Russia in the eighteenth century. The kingdom of Poland had been divided among three European countries but Russia took the largest share, including the capital, Warsaw. Many of the people of the western lands were Roman Catholics, but there were also a large number of Jews, who had always been persecuted by the Great Russians and forced to live within the 'pale', a narrow strip of western Russia.

In the nineteenth century nationalist movements grew up among the minority peoples, who demanded greater freedom and the right to practise their own religions and use their own languages. Pobedonostsev's answer was Russification, or enforcing the ways of life of the Great Russians on the minorities. Special privileges were given to those who followed the Russian Orthodox faith and those who spoke Russian. Schools which taught minority languages were closed. Opponents of Russian rule were arrested and exiled by the *Okhrana*. Worst were the pogroms. Mobs of Russians were encouraged by the government to attack Jews or other minority people and to destroy their homes and businesses while the police made no effort to interfere.

THE RUSSIAN POPULATION FROM THE CENSUS OF 1897

Nationality	*Numbers*	*Percentage of Population of Empire*
Great Russians	55,650,000	44·3
Ukrainians	22,400,000	17·8
White Russians	5,900,000	4·7
Poles	7,900,000	6·3
Lithuanians	1,650,000	1·4
Letts	1,400,000	1·1
Esthonians	1,000,000	0·8
Finnish people	2,500,000	2·0
Germans	1,800,000	1·4
Roumanians	1,100,000	0·9
Jews	5,000,000	4·0
Georgians	1,350,000	1·0
Armenians	1,150,000	0·9
Caucasian mountaineers	1,000,000	0·8
Iranians	1,000,000	0·8
Tatars	3,700,000	3·0
Kirghiz	4,000,000	3·2
Other Turkish people	5,750,000	4·7
Mongols	500,000	0·4
Others	200,000	0·2

2 Lenin and the Bolsheviks

Under the reaction it became much more difficult for the terrorists of the People's Will to carry on. Alexander Ulyanov was one of many who lost their lives at this time. Vladimir was luckier, escaping with a sentence of exile from Kazan. He was determined not to let this interrupt his study of the law and he carried on by himself, living at home with his mother and sister. Nor did his exile from Kazan stop him thinking, reading and holding discussions with friends about the future of Russia.

As time went on, however, Vladimir began to doubt whether the People's Will group was following the correct path. They believed in assassination, but every time a high official, or even a Tsar, was killed he was immediately replaced by a man of the same type. Terror only changed the men at the top; it did not alter the system under which Russia was governed.

He began to wonder whether the Liberals and the People's Will groups could show the way to a better future for the whole Russian people. The changes they wanted in Russia did not go deep enough. When a famine struck the countryside and starving peasants flocked into the town, Vladimir poured scorn on the committee set up to give them help. The wealthy citizens were doing this only out of 'saccharine sweet sentimentality', he scoffed. Most of them were liberals, who were prepared to give charity but not to lose their own wealth and privileges. They were just as great an obstacle to a better life for the poor as was the Tsar and his government.

These new ideas Vladimir had taken from the works of the German revolutionary, Karl Marx.

Marxism

Karl Marx had been an active revolutionary in the 1840s, one of many men trying to bring about the overthrow of the autocratic princes who had then ruled Germany. He had had to

St Petersburg in 1869

flee to England where he spent the rest of his life. Here, in wondering why his own revolutionary work had been unsuccessful, he worked out his idea that the key to understanding history and politics lay in the class struggle.

At every time in history, he argued, one class controlled the lives of the members of the other classes. In the feudal period it was the landowners who dominated. When society moved to the point where trade and industry replaced farming as the chief way of producing wealth, then the new ruling class were the capitalists. These were the men who had the capital, or funds, necessary to set up in business and give work to other people. The capitalists had as their allies the politicians, journalists, lawyers, bankers and so on who made up the *bourgeoisie* or middle class.

So, in the struggle against the landowning class, the real gainers were the capitalists, not the poor. As industry developed, the peasants were turned into the working class, or *proletariat*. The proletariat was exploited by the capitalists, who had the power to keep wages down to the barest minimum.

Many working men hoped that they could bring about better conditions by forming trade unions and socialist organizations. Marx, however, thought that the condition of the proletariat would worsen to the point where workers rose in revolution. To prepare the way for the coming proletarian revolution, Marx, and his friend Friedrich Engels, set up the Communist

21

International, a league of working men throughout Europe who would take the lead in explaining the theory of the class struggle to their fellow workers and prepare them to rise in revolution.

Marx believed that the Communist revolution would come in the countries of western Europe where the growth of industry had led to a sharp class struggle between the bourgeoisie and the proletariat. He saw little chance of revolution in a country such as Russia, where most of the poor were peasants. But Vladimir believed he saw signs that Russia was changing.

In 1864 Russia had produced fifteen million *puds*[1] of pig iron; in 1894 she was producing ninety-eight million puds. In the same period the amount of cotton cloth produced in factories had increased fifteen times. The growth of the textile and iron industries led to other changes. Railway mileage doubled in the 1890s. More important, a few towns had become huge centres of industry. St Petersburg, Moscow and Lodz (in Poland) all had huge new suburbs where miserable homes clustered round new factories. Into these towns flocked the peasants to find work. Often, whole families were forced to live in long wooden barracks, separated from their neighbours by only a sack screen. In some cases workers actually slept in the same room as their machines.

Mining centres grew up where no town had existed before. In the basin of the river Donetz a completely new industrial region was created, based on the nearby coal and iron fields. It centred on the town of Yusovka, named after a Welshman, John Hughes, who founded the New Russia Ironworks there. Most of the workers were peasants who came without their families. Sleeping in bleak wooden barracks, they worked long hours, suffered the misery of separation from their families, got drunk easily and had no other relaxation to relieve the unhappiness of their lives.

Vladimir noticed that 'the Russia of the wooden plough' was rapidly becoming the 'Russia of the steel plough and the threshing machine, of steam driven flour mills and looms'. These changes meant that Russia now had a force of nearly three million working men who could be made into the spearhead of a new revolutionary force.

[1] A *pud* is equal to thirty-six pounds.

Miners at work

By the time he passed his law examinations he had completely broken with his friends in People's Will and become a Marxist. He was eager to join a group of Marxists which held meetings in St Petersburg and, in 1893, left his mother's home to go and work in the capital.

St Petersburg

The St Petersburg Marxist group was one of several which had been set up in different parts of Russia to read and discuss the works of Karl Marx. To the police their activities seemed harmless enough and they decided to leave them alone. 'A small clique', said the police chief. 'Nothing will come of them for fifty years.'

Vladimir made a strong impression on his new comrades because of his energy and seriousness. Although he was only twenty-four they jestingly called him 'the old man'. One of them described him: 'His face was worn; his entire head bald except for some thin hair at the temples, and he had a scanty red beard. His squinting eyes peered slyly from under his eyebrows.'

Although they never warmed to Vladimir, they recognized him as their leader because of his strong will. For a short while he went abroad to talk to Russian Marxists in exile in France and Switzerland. They, too, were impressed and one described him as 'Ulyanov, future leader of the labour movement.'

In December 1895 the police decided that Ulyanov was dangerous after all. He had taken the lead in setting up the League for the Liberation of Labour to spread Marxist ideas among the working men of St Petersburg. He was arrested and sentenced to two years in prison and three in exile in Siberia.

Prison did not stop his activities. He was allowed to borrow books and have writing paper and pens but, of course, all his letters were read by the gaolers. He kept in touch with his friends by writing between the lines of letters and books, using milk as 'invisible ink'. For inkwells he used hollowed out cubes of black bread which could be swallowed in an emergency. One day he ate six.

In Siberia, Ulyanov was allowed to live freely in a peasant's hut. From there he wrote a great number of letters to his friends in St Petersburg and European Russia. Other exiles in the district visited him and spent long hours discussing the future work of the Marxists. Most of his time, however, was spent in writing a book, *The Development of Capitalism in Russia*, in which he showed how fast Russia was changing into an industrial state.

In 1898 a young schoolteacher, Nadezhda Krupskaya, who had worked with Ulyanov in St Petersburg, was arrested. She persuaded the police to allow her to join him in exile and very shortly afterwards they married. She acted as Ulyanov's secretary, copied out the greater part of the ten million words that he wrote in his life-time and shared all the difficulties and hardships of the years that lay ahead.

Not long after their marriage, Ulyanov wrote a revolutionary pamphlet and signed it 'Lenin', the name he kept for the rest of his life.

The Social Democratic Party

In 1900 Lenin and Krupskaya were freed and headed eagerly back to western Russia. Two years before, several groups of Marxists had founded the Social Democratic Party which was to be 'the class movement of the organized working masses'.

Above: Ulyanov (centre) with
other members of the League
for the Liberation of Labour

Nadezhda Krupskaya

Lenin soon realized that the Party was split. On the one hand were men who believed it most important to help workers fight for better wages and living conditions. They were not interested in revolution. On the other side were those who argued that the working class must see itself as the spearhead of revolution against the Tsar.

Lenin quickly decided he was on the side of the revolutionary Marxists and that he would lead them in a struggle to win control of the Social Democratic Party. The first step was to persuade the Party to appoint him and two others as editors of its newspaper, *Iskra* (The Spark).

It was impossible to publish in Russia so they left for Germany. In December 1900 the first issue appeared. Lenin wrote: 'Not a single class in history has reached power without thrusting forward its political leaders . . . capable of directing and organizing the movement. We must train people who will dedicate to the revolution, not a spare evening but the whole of their lives.'

He made *Iskra* the centre of a movement to train the sort of revolutionaries he wanted. From Germany he organized a whole network of agents throughout Russia. A Swiss Marxist invented a glue which would stick many copies together to make a board which could be made into packing cases or even suitcases, but which quickly came unstuck in a bowl of water. A special waistcoat was designed which would hold three hundred copies. Smugglers brought the papers into Russia by hundreds of different routes through Germany and Finland. Despite the precautions, many were captured and sent to Siberia.

Inside the country Lenin's agents distributed them far and wide. This was known as 'sowing'. Copies were handed out in factories, posted on street walls at night and even flung into the audience from theatre balconies. But sowing was not so important in Lenin's eyes as propaganda. He encouraged his agents to meet in 'cells' or small groups where they discussed the best means of spreading revolutionary ideas among the workers and where they made plans for building larger and stronger party groups. He kept close control over these cells, writing streams of instructions which were taken in to Russia by the *Iskra* smugglers.

The Secret Police, of course, could not remain unaware of the work of the Social Democrats for long. In April 1902 they reported on the activities of one of Lenin's agents:

'In Autumn 1901 the Social Democratic Committee of Tiflis sent one of its pupils, Joseph Vissarionovich Djugashvili, formerly a pupil in the sixth form of the Tiflis Seminary, to Batum for the purpose of carrying on propaganda among the factory workers. Social Democratic organizations began to spring up in all the factories of Batum. The results of the Social Democratic propaganda could already be seen in 1902, in the prolonged strike in the Rothschild factory and in street demonstrations.'

STALIN

Joseph Vissarionovich Djugashvili was arrested as a result of this report. He was the son of a worker in a shoe factory who had died when Joseph was eleven. His mother, a washerwoman who could neither read nor write, had worked and saved so that he could stay at school until, at fifteen, he had won a scholarship to Tiflis Seminary. This was a training school of the Russian Orthodox Church where discipline was extremely strict and almost every minute of the students' lives was closely controlled by the monks. The students were Georgians, but the monks were Great Russians and believed that it was their duty to train priests who were devoted to Russian traditions and loyal to the Tsar. The books that the students read were censored and reading anything other than religious or ancient Russian literature was forbidden.

Joseph very soon rebelled against the bleak life and the harsh punishments. He secretly got in touch with a group of Georgian nationalists in Tiflis. He attended their meetings and wrote poetry for their journal. He smuggled forbidden books into the seminary and read them secretly. Some of these were socialist writings and led him to join an underground Social Democratic group in Tiflis; he stole out of the seminary to give lectures on socialism to workers' study circles.

Defiance of this sort could not go unnoticed for ever and, after three years, Joseph was expelled from the seminary. He now gave all his time to working as a socialist agitator, helping to organize workers' groups, encouraging strikes, writing articles for illegal newspapers. He followed the debates between

Stalin, a photograph taken in 1917

Trotsky, a photograph taken in 1929

the different groups in the Social Democratic Party and decided that he was on the side of Lenin and the revolutionary socialists. By 1902 he was well known in many parts of Georgia as 'Koba', an active agent for the Social Democrats. It was at this time that the police arrested him and exiled him to Siberia. In 1904 he escaped and returned to carry on the work in Georgia. Some years later he changed his alias from Koba to 'Stalin', the man of steel.

In the year of Koba's arrest, 1902, Lenin moved the *Iskra* offices to London, because their German printers refused to run the risk of printing the paper any longer. Here he was joined by another young revolutionary, Leon Trotsky.

TROTSKY

Trotsky's real name was Leon Bronstein. He was the son of a poor Jewish farmer from western Russia and would probably have remained uneducated but for a cousin who gave him a home in the port of Odessa and sent him to school there. He proved to be a brilliant boy who could have succeeded in any career he chose, but his main interest lay in the writings of Karl Marx and other socialists. At the age of seventeen, with a few friends, he formed the South Russian Workers' Union. The idea was their own; they knew no adult Marxists or working-men's leaders. Nor, at first, did they know any workers. What made the South Russian Workers' Union a success was Bronstein's paper, *Our Cause*, which he wrote and printed himself. It was obvious that he had a gift for putting forward political ideas in a simple clear style.

The Union was successful and the paper was widely read. The police, of course, soon learned of it and, at nineteen, Bronstein was arrested and sent with his wife to Siberia. Here he continued his writing, and helped to organize the railway workers of the Trans-Siberian railway into Social Democratic groups. Eventually he escaped from Siberia, with a forged passport in the name of Trotsky—the name of the chief gaoler in one of the prisons he had passed through. He kept this name for the rest of his life.

It was about this time that his writings came to the notice of Lenin, who sent for him to come to London to work for *Iskra*.

The Party Splits

In London Lenin wrote his pamphlet *What is to be done?* In this he attacked those Social Democrats who favoured building up a mass party from the factory workers. Mere trade unionism was not enough, he argued, for trade union leaders all too easily accepted the need for a middle-class government. He believed that the first task of the Social Democrats was to build up a leadership of revolutionary intellectuals; men who were prepared to devote their whole lives to studying and preparing for the Socialist revolution. He himself had begun to lead the Party in this direction through the *Iskra* organization.

There were many Social Democrats who violently disagreed with Lenin and the quarrel came to a head when the party leaders met for their second Congress, or conference, in 1903. The first meetings were held in Brussels but they were soon driven out, partly by fleas and rats in their meeting place in a deserted warehouse and partly by the Belgian police. The Congress moved to London.

It was an angry and bitter meeting. They were divided on every point, particularly over the question of how the Party was to be organized. By a narrow majority, Lenin's group won a vote which decided that all the separate groups in the Party should disband and their members should obey only the orders of the Central Committee of the Social Democratic Party. After their defeat in this debate, many of his opponents walked out.

From this moment there were really two Social Democratic parties. Lenin's supporters became known as 'Bolsheviks' (from the Russian word for majority—*bolshinstvo*) because they

Living conditions for Russia's new working class. Houses in a small Russian town, 1895

The Tsar's home at Tsarskoe Selo, near St Petersburg

had a majority at the Congress, and those who believed in a Party which included trade unions and other semi-independent groups were called Mensheviks (from *menshinstvo*, or minority). In fact these labels were not correct. The Mensheviks had by far the largest support among the workers of Russia. Trotsky at this time took the side of the Mensheviks. He claimed that Lenin's idea of a small leadership of full time revolutionaries was more likely to lead to the setting up of a dictatorship over the working class than to be a means of helping workers fight their capitalist enemies.

Even some Bolsheviks feared that Lenin wanted to be a dictator and, for a time, he was out of favour and dismissed from the editorship of *Iskra*. He fought back through a new paper, *Forward*, and by 1905 was once again the head of the Bolsheviks. But this quarrel had lost the Bolsheviks many supporters and they were a tiny, weak party when the news came that revolution had broken out in Russia.

31

3 The 1905 Revolution

Nicholas II (1894–1917)
While the Social Democrats were arguing abroad, the threat
of Revolution inside Russia grew year by year. A new Tsar,
Nicholas II, had come to the throne in 1894. He was a pleasant,
charming man whose diaries are full of accounts of family
events, the weather and notes on country walks. But he completely failed to understand the new forces at work in Russia.
Like his father and grandfather he could not imagine any form
of government other than autocracy. He encouraged Pobedonostsev's reactionary activities and, after the Minister of the
Interior had been killed by terrorists, replaced him with
Plehve, a man described as 'the symbol of autocracy gone
mad'.

Pobedonostsev and Plehve gave the police even stronger
powers and organized bloodier pogroms against the Jews and
minority peoples. The result was simply to build up new
centres of opposition to the Tsar.

SOCIAL REVOLUTIONARIES
In the countryside Pobedonostsev did all he could to increase
the influence of the nobles. They were lent money to improve
their farms. Some were appointed to the new position of land
captain, and given the power to supervise the village *mirs*. This
seemed only a little short of restoring the powers that the
nobility had held over their serfs. The peasant reaction was
violent; murders and attacks on landlords increased. The
police and the Cossacks had to put down several serious risings
each year.

Peasants gave their support to a new party, the Social
Revolutionaries, formed in 1900 by a group of narodniks.
Most of the founders were students or intellectuals, but their
chief goal was to campaign for the transfer of nobles' land to
peasants. Branches of the Social Revolutionary Party sprang
up in thousands of villages. The belief in terrorist methods of

Nicholas II
with his wife,
Alexandra,
and his son,
Alexis

Paul Miliukov

the People's Will was still alive so a 'fighting organization' was set up to carry out sabotage and assassinations.

At the same time the liberal leaders of the zemstvos were building up their own party, the League of Liberation. This began as a protest against government interference. Zemstvo leaders had tried to hold meetings to discuss common problems but Pobedonostsev had forbidden them. Secretly a small group of angry liberals met in Moscow to work out a programme for limiting the power of the Tsar with a parliament. One of the League's leaders was Paul Miliukov, a great historian.

In 1904 leaders of the Social Revolutionaries and the League agreed that the moment had come to overthrow the autocracy. They had chosen a good time, for Russia was then at war with Japan.

The Russo-Japanese War

The war had been Plehve's idea. Driven to desperation by his failure to stop the opposition growing, he had decided that only one thing could save the Tsar: 'What we need is a short victorious war.' This was very unsound advice but unfortunately most of the Tsar's advisers agreed with Plehve and pressed for war against Japan.

For some time Russia had been increasing her strength in south-eastern Siberia. In the 1890s the first tracks were laid for the Trans-Siberian railway which was to run all the way from Moscow to Vladivostock on the Pacific coast. The Chinese territory of Manchuria jutted up into Russia and forced the railway into a 600-mile detour. In 1896 the Russians persuaded the Chinese to allow a railway to cross Manchuria and save the 600 miles. Two years later they forced the Chinese to lease them Port Arthur, a far better port than Vladivostock which was ice-bound in winter. In 1901, China allowed Russia to continue the railway as far as Port Arthur and to station Russian troops on Chinese soil to guard the line.

So far the only power Russia had interfered with was China who was too weak to resist. But over the border from Manchuria lay Korea, which was then occupied by the Japanese. They were alarmed at the possibility of the Russians trying to press their influence into Korea and were prepared to fight to defend

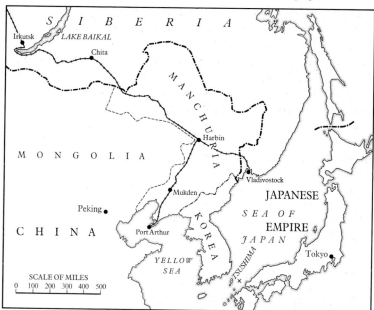

The Russo-Japanese War 1904–5

their possession. They first tried to arrange a settlement, but Plehve and his friends deliberately provoked war by treating the Japanese Prime Minister with great discourtesy when he visited St Petersburg. The Japanese made further patient attempts at negotiation. When these met with no reply, Japanese torpedo boats attacked the Russian fleet at Port Arthur in January 1904.

Many Russians saw Japan as a weak Asiatic nation such as China was at that time. They ignored the fact that, since 1868, she had been modernizing and modelling her industry, education and military training on ideas copied from western Europe. By contrast, Russia was an extremely backward state and the war was a complete disaster for her. Her armies were not properly supplied because a hundred mile section of the Trans-Siberian railway round Lake Baikal had not been completed, and goods had to be carried across the lake by ship, or by sledge across the ice in winter.

Although the troops fought bravely, the Russians were no match for the Japanese armies. They were forced to retreat

35

Above:
Russian
soldiers at the
time of the
war with
Japan

Plehve

from Manchuria. Port Arthur surrendered, even though there were still a million rounds and two months' supply of food left. The fleet based on Port Arthur had been defeated every time it put to sea and was finally destroyed in the autumn of 1904.

In a last desperate attempt to defeat the Japanese navy, the Russian Baltic fleet was sent half-way round the world to Japan. It left in October 1904 and after fantastic adventures, including the occasion when its drunken sailors fired on an English fishing fleet, reached the Sea of Japan in March 1905. There, in a fog, it ran into the Japanese fleet and was destroyed in forty-five minutes.

The news of this final blow forced the despairing Tsar to negotiate for peace. The war had been neither short nor victorious. For Plehve it was a disaster. In July 1904 he was killed by a terrorist's bomb.

The 1905 Revolution

The assassination was just one sign of the discontent that swept through Russia during the war. The backwardness of the country and the cruelty of the government, which had even tried to prevent the zemstvos organizing relief work, was seen at its worst. The army was badly equipped, its officers cruel and the medical services primitive. News of the soldiers' sufferings angered people already suffering from high prices and unemployment because of the war. The working men of St Petersburg and Moscow were in a rebellious mood.

Shortly before his death, Plehve thought he had found a solution to the unrest among the workers. This was to set up the Union of Russian Factory and Mill Workers. This was a trade union set up by the police to give them a chance to watch over the trouble-makers and revolutionaries among the workers. They hoped to avoid strikes and marches by encouraging workers to write petitions, which would give them a chance to air their grievances without becoming a danger to the government. At the head of the union was Father Gapon, a priest who was also a police agent. He was able to check the more violent and revolutionary workers until the hardships of the war grew so severe that they were no longer satisfied with polite protests.

In 1905 they organized a strike in St Petersburg's largest metallurgical factory, the Putilov works. Within a week it spread to other large factories. The strikers forced Father Gapon to lead a procession to the Tsar's Winter Palace. They carried a petition demanding the end of the war and a democratic government; the march was orderly and the strikers well behaved. Suddenly they were charged by cavalry. As they fled they were fired on from behind. Five hundred lay dead on the pavements and thousands more were wounded.

'Bloody Sunday' was a day of violence by the government. It was immediately answered by disorders throughout Russia. Work stopped in every large city as men came out on strike. In the countryside, Social Revolutionaries led the peasants to terrorism; landlords were murdered and their property destroyed. The Tsar's uncle was assassinated. The crew of the battleship *Potemkin* mutinied and sailed her away from the port of Odessa. Many of the minority nations made a bid for freedom from Russian rule. The Georgians revolted, broke away from the empire and declared themselves an independent state.

The League of Liberation seized its chance. Paul Miliukov organized the unions of doctors, lawyers and engineers into a powerful Union of Unions. The League, the Union of Unions and the zemstvo leaders decided to make a temporary alliance with the 'broad masses' of working people and their socialist leaders, to force the Tsar to give a parliament to the Russian people.

The opportunity came in the autumn after the news that a humiliating treaty had been signed with Japan. A strike broke out in the printing trade in Moscow. Within a week Russia was in the grip of the most complete general strike in her history. Every town was affected. Public services ceased; the postal and telegraph systems stopped work, no trains ran, bakers stopped making bread and shops, banks, even the law courts, were closed. The dancers of the St Petersburg ballet companies walked out.

In most cities *soviets*, or councils, of workers were elected by the men in each factory or trade. The Soviet committees took over the leadership of the strike. They organized essential supplies, arranged demonstrations, and published pamphlets

A painting of Bloody Sunday. Gapon and his followers are suddenly faced by troops
The crew of the battleship Potemkin mutinied and killed their officers in 1905

and posters. The government was powerless. No printers would work for the Tsar; many police thought it wise to go into hiding to avoid the revenge of angry citizens for past ill-treatment.

The most important soviet was that in St Petersburg. Its leading figure was Leon Trotsky who had hastened to Russia on the news of the revolution. Although he had worked for Lenin, he was now nearer to the Mensheviks than the Bolsheviks. Mensheviks had always held that the first task of socialists was to improve living and working conditions by building up strong socialist organisations and trade unions among the workers. The Bolsheviks believed that progress would only come after an armed revolution led by a small group of well-trained conspirators who need not be workers. Most of the St. Petersburg workers accepted a Menshevik point of view and it was they who were ready with the support and the organisation to set up the Soviet.

Lenin was much slower in returning to Russia and, when he did arrive, refused to give support to the soviets. He argued that the Menshevik leaders were not true revolutionaries and prophesied that they would allow themselves to be outwitted by the middle-class liberals, who only supported the strike for their own ends. He was proved right. The Tsar turned for advice to Witte, the man who had negotiated peace with Japan. Witte advised Nicholas that the only way to avoid civil war was to grant the parliamentary government demanded by the liberals. Reluctantly, Nicholas agreed and, on 17 October, an Imperial Manifesto announced sweeping changes. There was to be an elected parliament, or *duma*, and the autocratic government of the Tsar was to be replaced by a Council of Ministers led by a Prime Minister.

Witte was Russia's first Prime Minister. He had pressed the Tsar to grant the constitution. He now had to prove that this was the way to break the revolution, by splitting the liberals away from the socialists. The next six weeks saw a dramatic struggle between the St Petersburg Soviet and Witte. The Soviet sensed that people were tired of the strike and called for a return to work. But, to show their power, they organized a series of campaigns. One was for the end of the press censorship. This was a matter on which the liberals felt strongly and they supported the Soviet. Witte gave way and, for the first time in

A droshky, or horse-drawn cab

Russian history, the press appeared uncensored—although only for a few weeks.

The next campaign, for an eight-hour working day, was a failure. The soviets organized walk-outs from the factories at the precise moment when eight hours' work had been finished. In reply, the employers dismissed or locked-out their men. Employers' Associations were formed to fight the working men's demands. Most of their members were men who had been united with the soviets in the struggle for a constitution. Now the alliance of middle-class liberals and working men was at an end.

This was proved when the Soviet called for another general strike. Most factory workers obeyed the call but the clerks, public service workers and government officials stayed at their posts and the strike had to be called off. Now Witte felt strong enough to arrest the President of the Soviet. Promptly he was replaced by Trotsky and two other leaders. Five days later the Soviet headquarters were surrounded by troops and 270 members were arrested. Their last act was to smash their pistols so they should not fall into the hands of the police.

This was really the end of the 1905 revolution, although it was some months before the government troops had put down all the peasant risings and defeated the people of Georgia, who were brought back into the Empire.

4 Lenin in Exile 1906–17

The Dumas

In the spring of 1906 voting took place to elect the deputies, or members, of the Duma. Even before they met it was clear that the Tsar had broken his promise to share power with this first Russian parliament. He announced: 'To the Emperor of all Russians belongs supreme autocratic power. Submission to his power . . . is commanded by God himself.'

Lenin had always believed that the Duma would be a sham parliament and persuaded the Mensheviks and Bolsheviks not to take part in the elections. But even without socialist candidates, the elections produced a Duma made up of the Tsar's enemies. Most of the members were either liberals (who formed the Constitutional Democratic or Cadet Party) or Social Revolutionaries.

At the first meeting they demanded a full share in the government, the transfer of nobles' land to the peasants and the freeing of all political prisoners. After some days' delay they got the Tsar's answer. Everything they had asked for was 'inadmissible'. They continued to press for changes and to criticize the

The trans-Siberian railway

Tsar until one morning they arrived to find the meeting hall surrounded by troops and a notice on the door announcing that the Duma had been closed.

A second Duma was then elected. Lenin agreed that Social Democrats should stand for election. Only a few were successful; the rest of the Duma was again made up of liberals and Social Revolutionaries. Yet it was Lenin who provided the Tsar with the excuse for dismissing the second Duma after only three months.

He and his Bolshevik comrades tried to build up revolutionary groups, particularly in the army. Every move was watched by the police, who sent agents to join the Bolsheviks and pretend to encourage them. One reported: 'I met every member of the Central Committee then in St Petersburg, and all the members of the military organization; I knew all the secret meeting places and passwords of the revolutionary organization in the Army. . . . All the information I gathered was conscientiously reported to the Okhrana.'

With this information in their hands, the Okhrana arrested the Social Democratic members of the Duma. It was, in fact, a frame-up, for most of them were Mensheviks and had nothing to do with Lenin's wild and impossible schemes for revolution. The Okhrana and the government knew this but they needed an excuse for dissolving the second Duma. Lenin had played his part in killing the attempt by the liberals and the Mensheviks to establish a parliamentary government in Russia. When the third Duma met it was an entirely different body, for the Tsar had altered the election arrangements to give far more weight to the vote of landowners, who were not likely to elect his opponents. It was not, therefore, surprising that the third and fourth Dumas each lasted for five years.

Lenin in Exile

After the Okhrana had released details of his revolutionary plans, Lenin had to flee once again from Russia. He and Krupskaya were to spend the next ten years in cheap lodgings in nearly every country of Europe. In 1907 Trotsky escaped. He had been exiled to north Siberia, and taken there with other prisoners in a convoy of forty sleighs carrying a heavily armed guard. When the convoy had reached a point 1,000 miles from the nearest railway and 800 from a telegraph station, he made a bid for freedom. Dressed in two fur coats, fur stockings and boots, fur cap and fur gloves and carrying bottles of vodka to keep out the deadly cold, he made his way through the snow back to European Russia and over the border into Finland.

Lenin and Krupskaya were joined by other Social Democrat fugitives, for back in Russia the revolutionary and socialist movement had collapsed. In 1905 three million men had gone on strike, in 1906 there were only one million and by 1909 the number had fallen to 64,000. In the same five years the members of the different revolutionary and socialist groups fell from 100,000 to 10,000. In one of her letters Krupskaya complained, 'We have no people at all.' In 1909, Stalin, who had been arrested and exiled, escaped. On his way back to south Russia he called in at the St Petersburg headquarters of the Bolsheviks. He found that what had once been a powerful party with a membership of 8,000 had fallen to a group of less than 300.

The question of the right way to rebuild the movement was debated hotly by the exiled socialist leaders. Lenin was still convinced of the need to train revolutionaries and build up a network of underground revolutionary cells. The Mensheviks, on the other hand, argued for open propaganda among factory workers and in the trade unions.

Many men in both groups wanted them to merge and co-operate, and Trotsky, who belonged to neither, made many efforts to bring the Bolsheviks and Mensheviks together. The man who was always against co-operation was Lenin. Once a split had taken place, he said, it was the duty of those remaining to carry on a 'fight of extermination' against those who had broken away.

He often quarrelled with his own Bolshevik Party and ignored decisions made at their conferences. One visitor to a Bolshevik meeting heard complaints about Lenin on every side: 'He is one man against the whole Party. He is ruining the Party. How fortunate the Party would be if he disappeared, vanished, evaporated, died.' She asked one of Lenin's critics how he could keep the leadership against so much criticism, and received the reply: 'Because there is no other man who thinks and dreams of nothing but revolution twenty-four hours a day.'

Lenin did more than dream of revolution. He gave a lot of attention to organizing it. To build up the party funds, he set up the 'technical commission' whose task it was to organize robberies and hold-ups in Russia. He gave these raids the name of expropriations or 'exes'. The 'technical commission' was headed by an engineer skilled in making bombs. In 1906 he provided the weapons for a hold-up in the main streets of Moscow. Four guards were disarmed and the Bolshevik funds profited by 875,000 roubles. There were other raids in Moscow and St Petersburg but the main centre of activity was in the Caucasus, in south Russia.

The Bolsheviks could hire men from the bandits who infested the Caucasian mountains. Here, too, they had a loyal agent, Joseph Stalin. Stalin was little known outside south Russia, and he had taken no part in the theoretical arguments between the Bolsheviks and Mensheviks, but he had become known to Lenin as a capable organizer. He had twice called Stalin secretly to Finland to plan Bolshevik raids in the Caucasus. Between 1905 and 1908 there were 1,150 robberies and terrorist attacks. The most famous of these was the 'ex' of June 1907 in Tiflis. As a coach guarded by two policemen and five soldiers crossed the main square, seemingly innocent bystanders suddenly straightened up and hurled bombs, killing three of the guard and wounding about fifty bystanders. Another bomb thrown at the horses' legs stopped their panic-stricken flight. 341,000 roubles were seized and transferred to another coach. They ended up in Europe. In December, Lenin named the day when his agents should change the money at banks all over Europe. Most of them were arrested, for the Russian police had circulated the numbers of the stolen notes. The scandal was known in every city of Europe and it cost the Social Democrats a tremendous amount of sympathy. The Mensheviks were furious and so were most of the Bolsheviks. Only Lenin and a few close associates felt no shame.

Indeed, he renewed his attacks on the Mensheviks, the 'liquidators' of the revolution as he called them. By 1912 this second round of struggles for the leadership was over. The

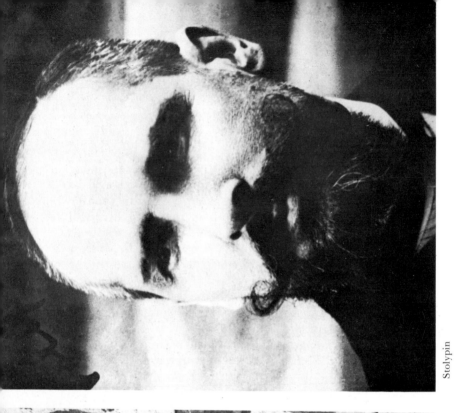

Stolypin

Stalin's country. Mountains near Tiflis in Georgia

Mensheviks broke off all contact with the Bolsheviks. Then Lenin and his supporters, who had set up a group called the Bolshevik Centre, declared themselves to be the Central Committee of the Bolshevik Party. The other Bolsheviks were not strong enough to oppose Lenin, who strengthened his position by issuing a new party newspaper, *Pravda* ('Truth'). At last he had the absolute leadership of the Bolshevik Party and he never again lost it. But in the struggle he had lost many supporters and gained many enemies among the revolutionaries.

Stolypin

The situation inside Russia gave Lenin little hope. The Tsar had disliked Witte, whom he thought too liberal, and replaced him by Stolypin in 1906. He favoured Stolypin for the sternness and cruelty with which he dealt with revolutionaries, Jews and Poles. More than a thousand were executed during his first year of office. But Stolypin was also an intelligent man, who realized that it was better to take steps to prevent revolution breaking out.

He did a great deal to encourage the development of industry. In four years the output of iron and steel rose by fifty per cent and other industries followed suit. This meant, of course, less unemployment and less discontent among the workers. Far more important were his plans to tackle the discontent among the peasants. 'The government', he said, 'relies not on the drunken and the weak but on the sober and strong, on the sturdy individual landowner.'

He ended the laws which forbade the peasant to move from his village, abolished the Land Captains, and set up a Peasants' Land Bank which provided loans for them to buy off their neighbours. The last was most important for it enabled a small proportion of the peasants to become Kulaks, or rich peasants who, Stolypin hoped, would support the government.

Nothing alarmed Lenin more than the success of Stolypin's land programme. From exile he described it as a race. If the programme had enough time, he feared, 'the stronger peasants will acquire almost all the allotments of land . . . and the chance of the revolution being helped by outbursts of revolution in the countryside would be lost. . . .'

An earlier attempt to kill Stolypin. Thirty people were killed when a bomb was thrown into his St Petersburg home

The Okhrana came to Lenin's aid in 1911. Stolypin had been under a great deal of criticism from people who thought he was giving way to liberalism. The Tsar, too, had turned against Stolypin, and, knowing this, the Okhrana did nothing when they learned of a plot to murder him. He was shot four times in a box at the theatre in full view of the Tsar.

The Road to War

The murder of Stolypin removed the only man with enough imagination to prevent another outbreak of revolution. Yet the country might have accepted the Tsar's autocratic rule for many more years if it had not been for the outbreak of World War One in 1914.

In the years before 1914 Russia had gradually drawn closer to France and Britain, who were to be her allies. Some of the Tsar's advisers would have preferred friendship with Germany, but this became impossible because the two powers were rivals in two vital areas. The first was Turkey. Russia had long claimed the right to interfere in the affairs of the Turkish empire which controlled the entrance to the Black Sea. Since 1908, when a revolution had taken place in Turkey, the Germans had gained the upper hand in Constantinople. The second area of rivalry was the Balkans, where both the Russians and the Austrians, who were allied to Germany, tried to influence the affairs of the small powers. In 1914 the heir to the Austrian throne was shot dead during a tour of Bosnia. The murderer was a Serb and the Austrians seized the chance to declare war on Serbia, an ally of Russia. In reply the Russians mobilized their armies, ready to fight both Austria and Germany. War broke out on 1 August 1914.

For a short time the war united the Russian people. The Tsar appeared in St Petersburg and swore he would not make peace until complete victory had been won. The crowds fell on their knees and sang 'God save the Tsar', as it had never been sung before. In the Duma, members made extravagant speeches offering their support in the struggle. There was an outbreak of hatred for everything German and the German Embassy in St Petersburg was attacked. The name of the capital was changed to Petrograd because St Petersburg was thought to

Nicholas II, holding an ikon or holy picture, blesses his troops

have too German a sound. No one was heard to complain when the sale of vodka was banned to prevent drunkenness.

The country was united for war and optimistic about the outcome. The western allies, Britain and France, were hopeful too. They had come to believe in the might of the 'Russian steamroller', the huge armies of the country of Europe with the largest population, which would force the Germans to withdraw more and more troops from the western front to meet the threat in the east. This was, in fact, what happened. The Germans marched on Paris, hoping for the immediate capture of the French capital. But, before they could make their final attack, they were forced to transfer part of their armies to meet the Russian advance.

Paris was saved, but the Russians were defeated. At the battle of Tannenberg, in east Germany, General von Hindenburg was faced by two Russian armies which together had far more men than he commanded, although his troops were better armed. He knew that the two Russian generals hated each other and took the risk of attacking one with his whole army. The gamble paid off; the second general was too slow in coming to support his rival, who committed suicide after seeing nearly all his entire army destroyed.

Lenin against War

In August 1914 Lenin was in a small Austrian village near the frontier with Russia. At any moment Russian troops might march through, and the peasants reported the strange behaviour of the bald Russian who had come to stay with his wife. The village policeman found a pistol and notebooks full of figures in Lenin's cottage. The figures were of agricultural production but the policeman took them for a spy's code. Lenin was arrested. He immediately telegraphed an Austrian friend, Dr Adler, who was a Socialist MP. Adler persuaded the government to free Lenin and allow him and Krupskaya to travel to Zurich in neutral Switzerland.

He arrived an angry and disappointed man. He believed that war was against the interests of working men and had expected the leaders of the socialist parties in Europe to refuse to support their governments when war was declared. This had not happened. Throughout July and August, socialists had met in every European country to discuss the coming war. In every case the Social Democratic or Labour Party had voted to support their government. Only a few individuals had stood out, such as Ramsay MacDonald, the secretary of the British Independent Labour Party, and Jaurès, the French socialist who was assassinated two days after declaring he would wage war against war.

In Russia most of the Mensheviks and some Bolsheviks decided to support the government in the fight against Germany. Lenin found himself at the head of a small group of anti-war socialists, and being accused of being a traitor to his own country. In September 1914 he wrote a pamphlet, *The Seven Theses on War*, in which he said that the Social Democrats should campaign for a socialist revolution even among the troops in the front line. He even went on to argue that, 'from the point of view of the working classes and of the toiling masses of all the Russian peoples, it was better that Russia not Germany should lose the war.'

When the pamphlet was read in Russia it led to the arrest of the five Bolshevik members of the Duma, who were exiled to Siberia. *The Seven Theses* were also read with interest by the German High Command. It would be very much to their advantage if Russia could be weakened by revolution. A German agent, Parvus, was sent to encourage the exiled revolutionaries. He had worked with Trotsky in the St Petersburg Soviet in 1905 but had later been expelled from the German Social Democratic Party for misusing funds. Working from a false 'scientific institute' in Zurich and a trading firm in Finland, Parvus gave funds to the exiles and smuggled their pamphlets into Russia.

· This did little harm to the Russian government. Neither did the Germans find Lenin an easy person to work with and soon they abandoned the scheme. So he spent 1915 and 1916 out of touch with Russia. He and Krupskaya had very few friends and little money. He worked in the public library collecting facts and ideas for another book, *Imperialism*. Very few people knew him and most of those he talked to in cafés were alarmed by his strange, nervous behaviour. Yet, in Russia, events were taking a course which would soon make his name the best known in Europe.

5 The End of the Russian Empire

The War, 1914–17

To fight in World War One needed more than huge armies. It was a struggle in which only nations whose forces were backed by large-scale heavy industry and modern transport could hope to be successful. Russia had neither. So the first campaign of the 'Russian steamroller' had ended in disaster at Tannenberg in 1914.

The following year the Tsar's armies suffered an even heavier defeat, and Poland and Lithuania had to be given up to the Germans. Russian casualties then stood at four million. In 1916 a brave attempt at recovery led to an attack on the weaker Austrian army. This was of great help to the allies, for it drew enemy troops away from the battle of the Somme, and also from the Italian front just in time to save the Italians from complete defeat. But again, Russian casualties ran into millions and their army had to retreat as the year ended.

The hardships suffered by the troops were terrible. By 1916, more than a third of all men of working age had been recruited into the army of fifteen million troops. A third of these had

Russian soldiers surrender to the Austrians, 1915

53

already been killed or wounded. Most of the officers were poorly trained and treated their men cruelly. One group of soldiers was heard to comment that 'when ten or fifteen generals are on the gallows we shall begin to win'. The Minister for War was said to have boasted that he had not read a military manual for twenty-five years. He believed in the bayonet in the age of the machine gun and heavy artillery. Arms were in short supply. At one point there was only one rifle to every ten soldiers and artillery guns were rationed to two or three shells a day.

The rest of the population suffered, too. The absence of

The Eastern Front in World War One

peasants from the land led to food shortages in the cities. They were made worse by the retreat of 1915 when Poland and Lithuania were abandoned. As the Russian armies retreated they drove the people of these areas before them and burned their crops and villages. The millions of refugees increased the grumbling against the government, as well as making the food shortage even graver. Workers and their families were hit by the rise in prices; 300 per cent since the beginning of the war, whereas wages had risen only 100 per cent.

The defeats and the hardships destroyed the support which the Tsar had had in 1914. In the Duma, the various parties came together to demand 'a government enjoying the confidence of the people'. The Tsar's reply was to close the Duma for a time and make himself Commander-in-chief of the armies.

This was unwise. He was no soldier and, still worse, he had to leave his wife, the Tsarina, to take charge of the government. She had little understanding of politics and refused to use any tact in dealing with her husband's opponents. She was also half-German and suspected of wanting to make peace with Germany. But she was distrusted mainly for the faith she placed in Gregory Rasputin.

Rasputin

Rasputin was a peasant from Siberia who had roamed over Russia as a 'holy man', claiming the power to make prophecies and heal the sick. In 1905 he came to St Petersburg and soon became the favourite of high society. The rumours of his power of healing spread to the Tsar and his wife, who grasped at this chance of help for their son, the heir to the throne. The young boy, Alexis, had been born with haemophilia—a terrible condition in which the sufferer's blood does not clot after an injury and any cut or bruise might lead to death from bleeding. The Tsar and his wife believed that Rasputin had some power over the boy and might be able to cure him of his illness, so, before long, he was established at court as a trusted adviser. In their letters they referred to him as 'our friend' or 'Gr.', short for Gregory. But Nicholas and Alexandra were probably the only people in Petrograd who believed in Rasputin's goodness and holiness. To most others he was something evil, and not only because he was dirty and slouched about in peasant's clothes. He was a drunkard and had a scandalous love life which even the gay nobility of Petrograd pretended to be shocked by.

None of this would have mattered if the monster had not used his influence over the Tsarina to replace the absent Tsar as the real ruler of Russia. It was on his advice that a game of 'ministerial leapfrog' was played. In less than two years, twenty-one ministers were dismissed and replaced by Rasputin's choices. There were four Prime Ministers in this period. The men he recommended were old, sick and unfit. They were reactionaries, but they pleased the Empress, who believed more strongly in the autocracy than her husband. She regarded him as weak and constantly urged him to be firmer in his dealings with the Russian people. When he went to the front, she urged, 'Don't yield. Be the boss. Obey your firm little wife and our Friend. Believe in us.'

Her advice united the nation against the Tsar and Tsarina. In the Duma, former supporters turned against Nicholas and took their lead from Miliukov, the liberal hero of 1905. In a bitter speech he attacked the Tsarina, reading out a long list of her mistakes and ending each with the cry: 'Is this stupidity or is this treason?'

Many noblemen lost faith in the Tsarina. Four of them, including two relatives of the Tsar, decided that Rasputin must be killed. The 'holy man' was invited to a party in the home of Prince Yusupov, where poisoned wine and cakes were laid out ready. He drank freely from midnight until after two, but the poison seemed to have no effect. In desperation, Yusupov went upstairs to borrow a revolver and then shot Rasputin. He appeared to be dead until he suddenly rose up and rushed at Yusupov who fled before him into a courtyard. Here Rasputin was shot twice more, but still refused to die. Yusupov, in a panic, battered his head with a steel bar and the body was then hastily thrown into the river.

The murder made the Tsar more obstinate. He ignored the Duma President and the British Ambassador when they warned him of the Empress's unpopularity. He took no notice when the police reported trouble in the town: 'Every day more and more of them demand, "Either give us food or stop the war".' This was in the grim days of January 1917 when ice on the railway lines stopped food supplies to Petrograd and bread queues became longer and angrier.

General Brusilov, perhaps Russia's best soldier, toyed with the idea of rebellion. 'If I must choose between the Tsar and Russia,' he said, 'I shall march for Russia.'

For the first time since 1905, the liberals in the Duma began to make close contacts among the socialists. The most important figure in this alliance was Alexander Kerensky. Kerensky was

Gregory Rasputin

a lawyer who, like Lenin, came from Simbirsk. He was not a Marxist, but had a great deal of sympathy for the poor workers and peasants and defended many revolutionaries free of charge.

The March Revolution

Even with so many men in the Duma and at court in agreement that great changes in the government were necessary, nothing happened until the people of Petrograd began to play their part. The first signs of trouble came on 4 March. Workers at the Putilov factory, where the revolution of 1905 had started, demanded a fifty per cent increase in wages. This was flatly refused and they struck. Four days later the management declared a lock-out, which meant that, not only the strikers, but all the 40,000 workmen at the Putilov factory were refused work. The strikers then formed a strike committee to bring out workers in other factories. Food was becoming scarce and there were angry scenes outside bakers' shops in the poorer parts of the town. In some cases women had broken into bakeries and stolen food. Cossacks were in the streets to help the police, who felt that the situation was about to get out of hand.

This was the day that the Tsar left to inspect his troops at the front. He believed that the food riots and strikes were no more serious than others in the previous years of the war. The men he left behind, however, sensed the coming trouble. The Duma pressed the government to provide emergency supplies of food to quieten the city. They also let it be known that they would not help the government to put down disorders unless Rasputin's ministers were dismissed.

The Prime Minister reported these demands to the Tsar by telephone. He also informed him that the disorders had grown worse and huge crowds were in the streets, some carrying red flags and chanting 'Down with the German Woman' (The Empress). The Tsar replied by telegram: 'I command that the disorders in the capital shall be stopped tomorrow.'

But they could not be stopped. The following day, 10 March, was Sunday and the crowds streaming from the poor districts to the centre of Petrograd were larger than ever. They clashed with the troops and sixty people were killed. After this, tempers rose still higher. The rioters attacked police stations, forced open gaols to release political prisoners and set fire to public buildings. Two regiments mutinied and refused to go into the streets to disperse the rioters. The President of the Duma telegraphed the Tsar describing the situation and saying that a change of government was necessary.

'The position is serious. There is anarchy in the capital. The government is paralysed. The transportation of food and fuel is completely disorganized. The general dissatisfaction grows. Disorderly firing takes place in the streets. A person trusted by the country must be charged immediately to form a ministry.'

Nicholas was still not going to take advice from the Duma. He put the telegram down with the words, 'Some more rubbish from that fat pig', and sent orders that the Duma was to be disbanded immediately. But the Duma leaders decided to disobey the Tsar and meet the next day. Some of them hesitated about taking such a step, but their minds were made up for them while they slept. All night the soldiers of the Vilinsk regiment were debating in their barracks. At dawn they marched out, led by a sergeant, with the band playing. They had decided to fight for the people against the Tsar. The mutiny spread to other regiments and by mid-day 25,000 troops had joined. The government dare not use the few troops who were still loyal for fear they too would mutiny rather than fire on their comrades.

In the Tauride Palace, the meeting place of the Duma, there was great confusion. No-one knew what was happening. Then Alexander Kerensky appeared. He had sent out friends to contact the leaders of the mutiny and had up-to-date information: 'I told them that there were riots all over the city, that the insurgent troops were on their way to the Duma and that I knew the revolution had begun. I said that as representatives of the people it was our duty to welcome them and to make common cause with them.'

Some of the Duma leaders were nervous at the thought of taking the lead in a revolution. The President exclaimed, 'I don't want to revolt.' But with 80,000 troops and strikers marching towards the Tauride Palace, Kerensky was in a strong position.

'I must know', he asked, 'what I can tell them. Can I say that the Imperial Duma is with them, that it takes the responsibility on itself, that it stands at the head of the movement?'

Above: the
Tauride
Palace,
meeting place
of the Duma

Nicholas
under arrest
after his
abdication

Eventually he persuaded them to let him go on to the balcony and announce that the Duma had set up a 'provisional government' which had taken over from the Tsar and his ministers.

The Tsar was unaware of what had happened. On the day of the revolution he had telephoned his wife who had told him that there was nothing to worry about. The next day, however, he was sufficiently alarmed to set out to join her. But it was too late. Railway workers blocked the line and he had to live out the last few hours of his reign in a railway carriage. At last he was ready to offer concessions. On the telephone to 'the fat pig' he offered to appoint a prime minister who was acceptable to the Duma. The courtyard of the Tauride Palace was filled with demonstrators and it was against the background of their cheering that Nicholas made out Rodzianko's reply, 'It is too late to make concessions: it is time to abdicate.'

Two representatives of the Duma were sent to get Nicholas to sign a document handing over the throne to his son, the sickly Alexis. But the Tsar refused to do this for, 'Alexis can never serve his country as I should like him to do. We have a right to keep him to ourselves.'

So Nicholas II gave up his throne in favour of his brother, the Grand Duke Michael. This alteration disturbed the Duma leaders. Most of them would accept as a king a boy who could not play any part in the government for many years. An adult member of the Romanov family would be no better than Nicholas. So Michael was offered the throne but told that the majority of the Provisional Government thought he should not accept it. Not surprisingly he refused and, on 16 March 1917, Russia became a republic.

A week later Colonel Nicholas Alexandrovich Romanov arrived at Tsarkoe Seloe to join his wife, the ex-Empress, and their children.

6 1917

The Soviet

The Provisional Government, made up chiefly of middle-class members of the Cadet Party, was formed at twelve o'clock on 12 March. By four o'clock it had a rival. As the revolution spread, trade union and socialist leaders, some only just released from jail, rushed to the Tauride Palace. There they immediately formed a Soviet which took over room 13 in the Palace. Most of them were Mensheviks and had a strong following among the workers. They remembered 1905, when the Soviet had collapsed after the Liberals had broken away from the socialists, and were determined that, this time, the working people and the soldiers who had made the revolution would gain the benefits.

They immediately took charge of Petrograd. Bank clerks asked them whether they should re-open the banks, railway-men were told which trains had to run, the city's food supplies and housing services were taken over. These actions gave them a strong position in the capital. Then, by issuing Soviet Order No. 1, they tried to make themselves the masters of the huge Russian Army. The Order laid down that troops should obey a soldiers' committee, elected by the men of each unit, which would follow the instructions of the Soviet in Petrograd. The committees were not to obey any order of the Provisional Government which contradicted a Soviet order. Order No. 1 went on to say that soldiers need no longer salute or stand to attention when talking to officers, who were to be addressed as Mr General, Mr Colonel and so on.

The real importance of Order No. 1 was that it was a sign that the Soviet and the trade union leaders did not trust the Provisional Government. For the next eight months they remained suspicious and watched every move of the government for signs that the middle-class liberals would break with the working-men's leaders as they had done in 1905.

The Provisional Government

Most of the members of the Provisional Government were liberals who sincerely wanted to turn Russians into free men. They immediately set about reforming the criminal laws. Judges were made independent of the government so that their decisions would be unbiased. The special courts of the secret police were abolished and policemen who had not gone into hiding were arrested. Political prisoners were released and soon were hurrying back from Siberia.

Other new laws made it illegal to persecute people from the minority nations and those who did not worship in the Orthodox Church. Poland was given her independence and special rights granted to the people of Finland.

The Soviets supported these reforms, but complained that nothing was done to improve the living and working conditions of the masses of the people. An act was passed reducing the working day to eight hours, but this did not help the unemployed. The chief failure of the Provisional Government was over the land question. A committee was set up to investigate ways of transferring land from the landlords to the peasants, but the government was too afraid of opposition from the nobles to take any action.

The greatest problem was, of course, the war. In 1917 Britain and France were hard pressed and felt they could only hold out if the Russians carried on with the campaign on the eastern front that had been promised by the Tsar before he was overthrown. The Provisional Government knew that the war was unpopular with the troops, who had thought the March revolution would bring an end to their miseries. It would also lead to food shortages and higher prices in the cities. Yet they decided to go on with it. They persuaded the Soviet to back this decision by promising that they would only fight a 'defensist' war and would not involve the troops in campaigns to win new lands for Russia.

The Soviet continued to mistrust the Provisional Government and to keep a careful watch on its actions. They were particularly suspicious of Paul Miliukov, the Cadet leader, who was minister of war in the Provisional Government. When he suggested that he did not accept the idea of a 'defensist' war they organized street demonstrations which forced the Prime

Kerensky at the front

Minister to dismiss him. He was replaced by the one member of the government for whom the Soviet had respect, Kerensky. Kerensky was a Social Revolutionary member of the Duma and also a member of the Soviet. Of all the ministers, only he was young enough and had enough revolutionary spirit to be more excited than frightened by what was happening. He had already strengthened the Provisional Government's position by travelling throughout Russia to address meetings of suspicious working men and peasants, who feared they would gain nothing by the revolution. Now he energetically set about reorganizing the army and building up the spirits of the troops.

The Finland Station

When the news of the March revolution reached Lenin in Switzerland, his first action was to telegraph to the Bolsheviks in Russia: 'Our tactics, absolute distrust, no support of new government, Kerensky particularly suspect, to arm proletariat only guarantee, no agreement with other parties.'

He feared that, unless he returned immediately, the Bolsheviks would make the mistake of supporting the bourgeois revolution of March rather than preparing for a second revolution of the proletariat. At first he thought of pretending to be a Swedish deaf-mute and travelling through Sweden on a forged passport. 'You'll fall asleep', Krupskaya told him, 'and see Mensheviks in your dreams, and you'll start swearing and shouting "Scoundrels, scoundrels", and give the whole plot away.'

There was another way. German agents approached the Bolsheviks, offering to arrange for them to travel through Germany, in the hope that they would reach Russia and cause trouble for the Provisional Government. Most of the exiles were not willing to accept help from the enemy, but Lenin argued, 'When the revolution is in danger, we cannot pay attention to silly bourgeois prejudices. If the German capitalists are so stupid as to take us over to Russia, it's their own funeral. I accept the offer, I go.'

He persuaded the Germans to agree that his party should travel in a separate compartment and that nobody should be allowed to approach them. In this way he hoped to keep the journey secret. But as the train left, other exiles stood on the platform shouting, 'Spies, German spies! Look how happy they are, going home at the Kaiser's expense.'

The party travelled through Germany by train, took a boat to Sweden and from there entered Finland. On the afternoon of 16 April, Lenin's train pulled up at the Finland Station in Petrograd. He was in his own country again after an exile of ten years.

Peace! Bread! Land!

A vast crowd had gathered to welcome Lenin. Banners waved and military bands played triumphant music. In the middle of the throng stood a nervous group from the Petrograd Soviet. They were worried that Lenin would attack the Soviet for its co-operation with the Provisional Government. Their leader made a speech saying they needed, 'not disunion but the closing of the democratic ranks'. Lenin, however, had already made up his mind. He was in Russia to teach the workers that the revolution of March was only the first step to the greater revolution of the proletariat.

Even some of the Bolsheviks were unsure at first about Lenin's policy. Stalin, for instance, had backed the Soviet when it supported the government's war policy. But he and other Bolsheviks soon came round when Lenin outlined his plan of action. They must first, he argued, arouse as much discontent as possible among the soldiers, workers and peasants. With the slogan, Peace! Bread! Land!, the Bolsheviks could show themselves as the only party which was campaigning for the things most wanted by the masses. As new elections took place for trade union leaders, army committees and the soviets, it would be Bolsheviks who were elected in place of the Mensheviks and Social Revolutionaries. At the same time Peace! Bread! Land! would weaken the government's position. Then, with a weak government and soviets controlled by Bolsheviks, it would be time, Lenin said, to bring into play his second slogan, 'All power to the Soviets'.

The quickest way to weaken the Government was to bring about a mutiny in the army. Bolshevik agitators were sent to work among the troops and Lenin sent a message: 'We summon you to a social revolution. We appeal to you not to die for others but to destroy others, to destroy your class enemies on the home front.'

Kerensky issued a reply on the same day: 'It's easy to appeal

Bolshevik demonstrators in Petrograd

to exhausted men to throw down their arms and go home, where a new life has begun. But I summon you to battle, to feats of heroism . . . to death; to sacrifice yourselves to save your country.'

For the last time the soldiers made the sacrifice. The offensive against the Germans and Austrians began on 18 June. By the end of the month the Russians were retreating before a much better equipped army. In Petrograd the news of the defeat came at a bad time. Food supplies were short again; the bread ration had been cut from one and a half pounds to one pound a day. The shortages led to further price rises; the end of the offensive meant that many men in munitions and arms factories lost their jobs. Everyone blamed the war. For several days the mood in the working class districts was angry and then the July Days rising broke out.

The July Days

The Machine Gun Regiment provided the spark, by marching with their weapons into the streets to demonstrate against the government. They were joined by sailors from the naval base at Kronstadt. Immediately afterwards the workers at the Putilov factory came out on strike. The streets on 16 and 17 July were crowded with armed men, as they had been in March. But this time, they were demonstrating not against the Tsar but the Provisional Government. Time after time the cry went up: 'Down with the Provisional Government. All power to the Soviets!'

They were shouting Lenin's slogan and demonstrating for peace and bread. But the July rising had come too early to suit Lenin's plan. If the government did fall and if power passed to the Soviets, it would be a Menshevik and Social Revolutionary group that took over. The Bolsheviks, however, realized that to keep their reputation as the party of revolution, they would have to take part, while trying to prevent the rising going too far. Trotsky saved a Social Revolutionary member of the government from a lynching; Lenin tried to calm down the Kronstadt sailors. But they failed to stop clashes with troops called in by Kerensky and 400 people were killed in two days.

Kerensky's firm action in calling in troops to fire on the demonstrators ended the rising. Although they had tried to prevent the July Days, it was the Bolsheviks who were blamed. The Provisional Government ordered the arrest of their leaders and published evidence which seemed to prove that Lenin was a spy in the pay of the Germans. Government troops occupied the Bolshevik headquarters and raided the *Pravda* offices, smashing the printing machinery. All over Petrograd they hunted down Bolshevik leaders. Trotsky gave himself up but Lenin went into hiding.

For two or three weeks he hid in a wood near Petrograd, sleeping in a haystack. During the day he wrote pamphlets, using a tree-stump as a desk. Then he shaved his beard and moustache, put on a blond wig and crossed into Finland, pretending to be the fireman on a locomotive. Eventually he arrived in Helsinki, where he stayed at the home of the Police Commissioner who had once been a worker in Petrograd.

From his hiding place, Lenin wrote letters to the press trying to prove that he was not a German spy. It was not difficult to show that the government's evidence was very weak and that some of the letters it had printed were forgeries. But since 1917, so much new evidence has been found that most historians think that Lenin did receive money from Germany. He was not, in any case, the sort of man who would refuse money from anyone if it would help his cause.

Kornilov

Kerensky's triumph did not last long. His reputation as a sympathizer with the socialists led many landowners and army officers to look on him as a weak prime minister. They believed that the socialists were responsible for Russia's troubles at home and for her defeats in the war, and wanted a man who would destroy the power of the soviets. The leader of this opposition was the Commander-in-Chief of the army, General Kornilov. Kornilov was a colourful character, always protected by a bodyguard of Asian soldiers dressed in red coats, but he had no political sense and was described as a 'man with a lion's heart but the brains of a sheep'.

He demanded that the Provisional Government should refuse to recognize Soviet Order No. 1, and that the railways and munitions works should be placed under military control.

The July Days

The forged passport with a photograph of Lenin in the disguise he used to escape to Finland

Fearing the anger of the Soviet, Kerensky refused. Kornilov saw this as a sign of weakness and decided to overthrow the Government and set up a tough military dictatorship. He moved troops close to Petrograd; officers within the city were ordered to be ready to arrest socialists when the word was given. Kornilov told his chief of staff: 'It's time to hang the German supporters and spies, with Lenin at their head and to disperse the Soviet of Workers' and Soldiers' Deputies so that it will never re-assemble.'

In September Kerensky learned of the plot and immediately dismissed Kornilov. Kornilov ignored him and ordered his troops to march on Petrograd. Kerensky was almost without friends. Even members of his own cabinet had known of the plot but had not reported it to him. His position seemed hopeless but he was saved by the Soviet. As soon as they learned of Kornilov's march they organized the defence of the city. Factories stopped work and men poured out to build barricades. Once again the sailors marched in from Kronstadt and took up their positions alongside soldiers loyal to the Soviet. A new force appeared, too. These were the Bolshevik Red Guards, bands of workers who had been armed by the Bolshevik leaders. Previously they had not dared to show their strength openly, but in this crisis they were welcomed and 25,000 Red Guards took up their positions in the path of Kornilov.

His troops never reached the city. Railwaymen interrupted his signals and sabotaged the railway lines. Bolshevik agents

Red Guards firing from an armoured car

then moved out among the soldiers and persuaded them to mutiny against Kornilov. Within a week his bid for power was over and he was fleeing to the south.

The Bolsheviks Seize Power

The Kornilov affair placed Kerensky at the mercy of Lenin and the Bolsheviks. Their popularity in the city soared because of the leading part they played in its defence. In many factories and army units the old delegate to the Soviet was replaced by a Bolshevik. By October the Bolsheviks had won enough seats in the Soviet to turn out the old Executive Committee, which had led the Soviet since March, and replace it with a new one on which there were twelve Bolsheviks but only six Social Revolutionaries and three Mensheviks. Trotsky was elected chairman, and for the next few weeks became a much more important figure than Lenin who was still in hiding.

As news of the part played by the Bolsheviks against Kornilov passed through the country, soviets in towns, villages and army units passed into their hands. They were helped by the outbreak of a new wave of peasant violence. When autumn arrived, and the Provisional Government had still failed to arrange for land transfer, the peasants took the law into their own hands. Nobles' houses were burned, landlords and their families murdered. In many villages, committees were set up to seize landlords' land and distribute it among the peasants. Many committees sent representatives to Petrograd to ask for help from the Soviet. Trotsky told them that 'We could only help if the government power were in our hands.'

Was this the time for a Bolshevik revolution? Lenin thought so and sent urgent messages from Finland. 'The question of arms', he wrote, 'is now the fundamental political question. ... We have *thousands* of armed workers and soldiers in Petrograd who could *at once* seize the Winter Palace, the general staff, the telephone exchange and the large printing establishments.' Many Bolsheviks, however, were more timid, and nervous at the thought of an armed revolution. Lenin, furious with those who believed 'that a wave will carry away Kerensky', returned to Petrograd, still in disguise. On 23 October he argued all through the night at a meeting of the Central

The Smolny Institute, Bolshevik headquarters in 1917

Committee of the Bolshevik Party. At dawn the resolution that was to change Russia's history was passed by ten votes to two: 'The Party calls for the organization of an armed insurrection.'

Trotsky became the organizer of the revolution, which was to take place under the slogan 'All power to the Soviets', because this now meant the same as 'All power to the Bolsheviks'. He worked from Room 10 in the Smolny Institute, the headquarters of the Bolsheviks. Room 10 was the office of the Military Revolutionary Committee, which issued arms to the Red Guards and drew up plans for taking key points in the city.

The Bolshevik newspapers openly declared that the revolution was to take place. Only the date was unknown. This was decided by the All-Russian Congress of Soviets which was to meet on 7 November. Lenin and Trotsky wanted to strike before its meeting, because they feared that some of the leaders of soviets outside Petrograd might hesitate to revolt and begin weeks of argument, which would give Kerensky time to call in support. So the revolution was to begin on the night of 6 November.

In the darkness of that night an American reporter, John Reed, found his way into the Smolny Institute and spoke to a Bolshevik: 'We're moving. We pinched the Assistant Minister of Justice and the Minister of Religions. They're down in the cellar now. One regiment is on the march to capture the Telephone Exchange, another the Telegraph Agency, another the State Bank. The Red Guard is out. . . .'

Kerensky awoke on 7 November to be told that the railway stations, the banks, power stations and the telephone exchange had all been seized. The chances of fighting back were almost nil. Soldiers and Red Guards held the bridges over the river, they had captured the arsenal in the St Peter and Paul fortress and the cruiser *Aurora*, manned by Bolshevik sailors, had its guns trained on the Winter Palace. He decided on a last desperate bid to break the revolution and left the city openly, in a car lent by the American Embassy, to find troops who would follow him to Petrograd. No-one tried to prevent him going. In some cases Bolshevik soldiers snapped into a smart salute as he went by. He found no loyal troops and before the end of the day Lenin, not he, was the ruler of Russia.

Throughout 7 November the Bolsheviks took over more of the city. There was little resistance, and by nightfall there was only the Winter Palace untaken. Here sat the members of the Provisional Government, protected by women soldiers and young officer cadets. At ten o'clock a few shots were fired from the *Aurora*, then soldiers and Red Guards rushed in. It took them some time to find their way to the room where the members of the government sat. They looked up when the door flew open and a little man burst in followed by soldiers. 'I inform

The Women's Battalion guarding the Provisional Government in the Winter Palace

you all, members of the Provisional Government, that you are under arrest. I am Antanov, chairman of the Military Revolutionary Committee.' One of the ministers replied, 'The members of the Provisional Government yield to force and surrender in order to avoid bloodshed.'

It was one o'clock in the morning of 8 November when the news reached the Smolny Institute, where the All-Russian Congress of Soviets was meeting. In one corner sat a blond man, his face half covered with a handkerchief. The handkerchief and wig were put away as Lenin went to the platform and spoke: 'Comrades, the workers' and peasants' revolution, whose need the Bolsheviks have emphasized many times, has come to pass . . . we shall have a Soviet Government, without the participation of a bourgeoisie of any kind. The oppressed masses will themselves form a government.'

7 Lenin in Power

Tenuous hold on power

The Dictatorship of the Proletariat

The Bolsheviks set up the Council of People's Commissars or *Sovnarcom*. Its chairman, the new ruler of Russia, was Lenin and there were fourteen other Commissars, or ministers. On every side they found opposition. The Bolsheviks were the smallest party in Russia and had only won control because of their support in the army. The liberals and Cadets were already building an anti-Bolshevik army to overthrow them; the Mensheviks and Social Revolutionaries were hardly any more friendly.

Like all Marxists, Lenin believed that, in the first period after a revolution, there must be 'a dictatorship of the proletariat', when the government, on behalf of its working-class supporters, had to take stern and cruel measures against counter-revolutionaries—the forces of the capitalist classes who would try to regain power. The dictatorship of the proletariat had to be carried out by the Bolshevik Party, or Communist Party, as it was renamed at this time. Lenin refused to ally with other socialists. Nor would he rule through the soviets, even though the Bolsheviks had seized power crying, 'All power to the Soviets!' *The problem of keeping power to himself*

In 1917 there were fewer than a quarter of a million Communists, but they were well organized and trained to accept orders from the party leadership. Most decisions were taken by the Political Bureau (or Politbureau) which was a committee of about a dozen leaders, most of whom were also Commissars in the government. Below them was the Central Committee, which was formed from representatives from all over the country, but this met so rarely that real power was left in the hands of the Politbureau.

Many of Lenin's comrades were horrified by the measures he took to keep the Communists in power. Only a week or two after the revolution, he decided to stop press criticism by banning all newspapers, except those published by the Party.

going against his revolutionary principles?

Lenin speaking in Moscow. Trotsky is standing on the right

In December 1917, he set up the extraordinary Commission against Counter-revolution, Sabotage and Speculation, always known as the Cheka. — *against her principles.*

In charge of the Cheka was Felix Djerzhinsky, a fanatical Communist who had spent most of his life in gaols and in Siberia. Now he was the chief of the new Russian secret police.

He built up a force of 30,000 men. Some were, like himself, honest men eager to work for the good of the country. Others were thugs who saw a chance to become local bullies. Before the end of 1918, the Cheka had executed 50,000 opponents of the Communists. But Lenin took the responsibility upon himself and defended the 'Red terror', arguing 'Do you really think we shall be victorious without using the most cruel terror. . . . If we cannot shoot a man who sabotages, a member of the White Guard, then what kind of revolution is this?'

Control over the vast areas outside Petrograd was difficult. As Trotsky said it had to be 'revolution by telegraph'. All the Politbureau could do was to telegraph instructions and hope they would be faithfully carried out. Eighty-five per cent of the Russians were still peasants and unless they supported the revolution it would fail. For this reason, Lenin's first act was to issue the Decree on Land which allowed village committees to seize nobles' land and share it among the peasants.

But even after they had won their land, the peasants remained suspicious of the Communist Party, which had grown up in the cities. They remained loyal to their own party, the Social Revolutionaries, who had put forward exactly the same policy on land as the Communists.

The Constituent Assembly

This was made clear by the results of the elections for a Constituent Assembly. The Assembly was a parliament which the Provisional Government had promised to call just before it fell. Believing they could win the elections, the Communists had decided to stand by Kerensky's promise. But 267 Social Revolutionaries were elected and only 161 Communists. Nevertheless the Assembly was allowed to meet in January 1918—for just one day.

The meeting was rowdy. Communists jeered the Social Revolutionaries; Red soldiers and sailors threatened them with their rifles. Despite the interruptions, the Social Revolutionaries pressed on to pass laws which were very much the same as decrees already made by the Communists. They refused, however, to recognize the Communists as the rulers of Russia. The next day they found the Assembly closed and soldiers barring the door. No parliament ever met again in Russia.

77

Street fighting between Bolsheviks and Social Revolutionaries, 1918

Early Reforms

The Communists used their dictatorship to force through changes which destroyed some of the oldest Russian traditions. One decree cut away the power of the Russian Orthodox Church, which had controlled much of Russian life and education and stood in the way of reform. All its land and wealth was confiscated. It was forbidden to teach religion and to carry out marriages, which in future were to be held in a civil court.

Other decrees altered the inferior position of women. They were declared equal with men, able to own property and sign documents without their husbands' permission. Anyone could obtain a divorce simply by asking for it. The Communists also changed the procedure in law courts to make it simpler to obtain justice. They abolished all ranks and titles and decreed that Russians were to be addressed only as Citizen or Comrade. It was at this time that the Gregorian calendar was replaced by the Julian or Western calendar.[1]

[1] See the explanation in the preface.

The Peace Conference at Brest-Litovsk. Trotsky stands second from right

ended the war but against principles.

Brest-Litovsk

There was little chance of any further reforms until the question of the war with Germany was settled. A team of negotiators, headed by Trotsky, was sent to meet the enemy at Brest-Litovsk in Poland. The Germans were in a very strong position and offered peace only if Russia gave up Poland, Lithuania and the Baltic states. One of the Russian team committed suicide when he heard these terms. The others returned to advise Lenin that they must continue with the war, but he was determined on peace: 'If war should break out again, our government would be wiped out and peace would be made by some other government. We must become strongly entrenched in power, and for that we need time.'

Lenin was proved absolutely right. When the Russians delayed signing, the German army advanced again. The Russians were unable to make any resistance and on 3 March 1918 the treaty of Brest-Litovsk was signed. As Lenin had foreseen, the conditions were even stiffer. Russia had to abandon not only

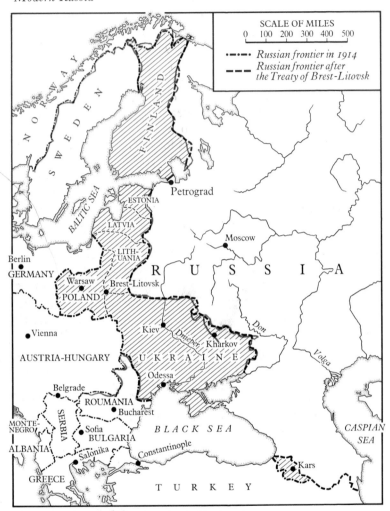

Russian Losses by the Treaty of Brest-Litovsk, March 1918

Poland and Lithuania but Finland, the Ukraine and parts of Caucasia. She thus lost one-third of her population, one-third of her agricultural land and more than half of her industry. Lenin, however, had no intention of keeping to the treaty longer than was necessary. When it was brought to him he said, 'I shall neither read it, nor carry out its terms whenever there is a chance not to do so.'

The Civil War

The Peace of Brest-Litovsk was a blow to the allies. Although the Russian armies had won no great victories in World War One, they had taken a lot of pressure off the western front. Now, unless something were done quickly, the German High Command would be able to transfer all its armies to the west for a crushing offensive. So the idea of intervention was born. British troops were despatched to Murmansk and Archangel in north Russia, and French troops to the Black Sea area in the south. At the same time Japanese[1] troops entered Siberia through Vladivostock. The allied governments' claim was that they were sending troops to Russia to wage war on Germany. But, in fact, it was impossible to do this without linking up with the anti-Bolshevik forces that were gathering strength.

There were many of these. A confusing mixture of Social Revolutionary, Menshevik, Liberal and Tsarist centres of resistance sprang up. Ex-army officers like Kornilov played an important part. The opposition, or White, forces, were helped by peasant discontent at the Communists' treatment of the Social Revolutionaries. They were joined by 40,000 Czech soldiers. These were men who had deserted to the Russians from the Austrian army. They were waiting to be taken to Vladivostock so they could sail to join the allies on the western front. But the Communists had held them up, and their tempers were frayed even more when Trotsky insisted they leave their weapons behind. At this point they mutinied and joined the White forces in Siberia.

At the end of 1918 the Communist government found itself occupying only a small fraction of Russian territory and there were another twenty governments operating in the country. The five most threatening of these were:

1 General Deniken's forces in the south. These were ex-Tsarist forces, backed by Cossacks and by a French army supplied through the Black Sea Ports.

2 The Omsk government, led by an ex-Tsarist, Admiral Kolchak. This controlled the area from Lake Baikal to the River Volga and had the support of the Czechs. Admiral Kolchak had been helped by the Allies and was recognized by them as the legal government of Russia.

[1] The Japanese had been allies of Britain and France in World War One.

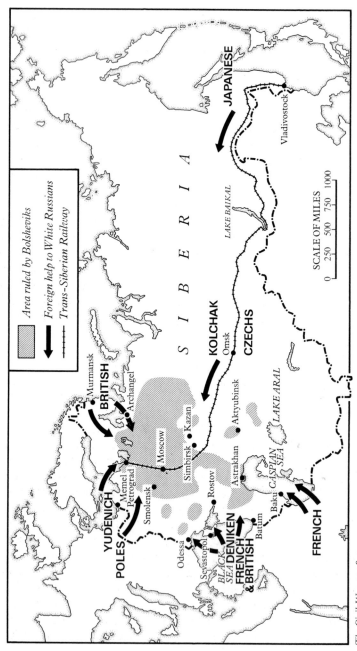

The Civil War 1918–21

3   Further east, a government, headed by a man who was little more than a bandit, was supported by the Japanese who held Vladivostock—an important supply route for the White armies.

4   In Archangel, a Socialist Revolutionary government which allowed the British to land troops.

5   In the north east, the Russian General Yudenich was preparing for an attack on Petrograd. He, too, had British support.

The anti-Communists held nearly all the food growing areas. Most soldiers had either returned home or deserted to the Whites. The munitions industry had broken down because of the shortage of supplies of raw materials. Many peasants hoped for a White victory. Lenin thought that Petrograd might easily fall to General Yudenich and ordered the removal of the government to Moscow. Here it took up its headquarters in the Kremlin where it has remained ever since. With savage energy Lenin and Trotsky, now Minister for War, worked to save the Communist Government. Two things were essential, to create a loyal Communist or Red Army, and to organize food and supplies in the country by a programme of War Communism.

The Red Army

Trotsky was constantly on the move, riding in his special train which carried a printing press, emergency supplies of ammunition, living quarters for his staff and a car in which he could visit the front line.

His first problem was to find enough trained officers. They did not exist among the Communists so he took the bold step of appointing officers of the old Tsarist army; 27,000 of them before the war was over. But there was a grave risk that they would lead their men over to the Whites, so each officer was placed under the orders of a political commissar who was, of course, a member of the Communist Party.

Even so there were many desertions, and not only by officers. Many of the soldiers conscripted into the army were weary of war and disliked the Communists. To prevent desertions, Trotsky recruited as many factory workers as he could. They were more ready to fight and die for the Red government, and regiments with a large number of Communist workers made the best fighting units. The weak-hearted were made to fight

Red Army soldiers

by terror. Special Cheka units followed them into battle and machine-gunned men who fled from the enemy. In this way Trotsky managed to build up an army just strong enough to defeat the Whites. This would not have been possible without War Communism.

War Communism

The Communists had never denied that they would put an end to private ownership and nationalize industries and trading concerns. But, immediately after taking power, they had seized only the most important of these—the National Bank, the electricity undertakings and large industrial firms like the Putilov metal works. The shortages of the Civil War decided them to nationalize all industries in the Red held area so they could be forced to produce the goods most needed to fight the war.

The workers lost their freedom. So many were leaving the towns where food was scarce that the Communists had to conscript them forcibly into industry. They were kept in their jobs by the need to own a worker's book. Without this, which showed their place of work, they could not get food, clothing, fuel or lodgings. At times the food shortage was so acute that the ration of bread fell to one ounce a day.

Even this was not available to members of the old ruling classes. They had no workers' books and the only way many of them could live was by selling their jewellery and furniture on the Black Market. After this was gone, many of them faced starvation unless they could leave Russia or try to leave the towns and eke out a living in the countryside like the family of Dr Zhivago. The Communists, of course, had little sympathy for these people.

The gravest difficulty was to provide enough food for the townspeople to give them even their tiny rations. The peasants were reluctant to part with their crops to the official government stores, which did not pay anything near the prices they could get by selling privately or on the Black Market. So teams of soldiers and Cheka men were sent to the villages to requisition grain. Usually this meant a search by armed men who took away all the grain and vegetables they could find, leaving only a little for seed and for the peasant's own needs. On many occasions, peasants who had returned from the army with their rifles and grenades used them against the requisition bands. The Communists claimed that it was only the Kulaks, or rich peasants, who were against them; but this was by no means true. There were many savage Red Terrors ordered by Lenin: 'It is necessary to organize an extra guard of well-chosen, trustworthy men. They must carry out a ruthless mass terror against the Kulaks, priests and White Guards. All suspicious persons should be detained in a concentration camp.'

It was in the summer of 1918 that the Cheka executed Nicholas II and his entire family so that they would not become the figure-heads of opposition to the Communists.

A few months later, there was an attempt on Lenin's life. He was shot by a woman, Fanya Kaplan, after speaking at a rally in Moscow. One bullet entered his neck and another his collar bone. He was unable to work for several weeks. Fanya Kaplan was shot, without a trial, by the Cheka three days after. She was followed by more than 500 suspected enemies of the revolution, many of whom were arrested simply because they were members of the bourgeoisie.

The Whites

Throughout 1919 the outcome of the war was never clear. At one point Admiral Kolchak's armies reached within 200 miles of Moscow. Yudenich's men were in the suburbs of Petrograd before they were turned back. But the Red Army slowly gained the upper hand. Kolchak was captured and executed at the end of the year. General Deniken's army retreated and was evacuated from the Crimea in early 1920. A new threat, by a Polish army, was beaten off in 1920. At the end of that year there was little more than mopping-up to do. The Reds had won the Civil War.

One of the reasons for the collapse of the Whites was the weakness of the allied help. When the World War ended in November 1918 there was no need to fight Germany from Russian territory. Some British and French politicians supported Churchill who argued that the Communist government should be strangled at birth. But more of them wanted to withdraw from Russia and demobilize their armies as quickly as possible. They knew they would face an outcry from the voters if they entered into another war. So in 1919 and 1920 most of the help which came to the Whites was in the form of arms and ammunition and not men, except for a few adventurers who did not really believe in the White cause. One soldier remembered: 'I was passing by B Company train and I heard someone ask Parker what he was fighting for. He said, "A quid a day".'

The Whites were divided among themselves. To gain power in the Omsk government, Admiral Kolchak's supporters murdered their Social Revolutionary allies. The government that Kolchak then established at Omsk was as bad as any that had held power under the Tsars. For this reason many people began to prefer the Reds. Admiral Deniken complained that his armies 'were followed by landowners forcibly re-establishing their rights. . . . The returning landowners brought back unrest by outrageously increasing the rent for holdings.'

The Whites, if anything, were crueller than the Reds and they paid the penalty by losing the war. They fled in large numbers to almost every country of the world:

'The men of the defeated White Army built roads in the Balkans, dug coal in Bulgaria, Belgium and France, worked in

Above: White officers training in England before returning to fight the Reds in Russia

A refugee White. A Russian princess works as a waitress in France

plantations in South America, took jobs as factory workers and field hands in countries all over the world. Generals shined shoes in Constantinople and opened cabaret doors in Paris. Princesses waited on tables in Berlin, Counts became blacksmiths and colonel's wives did needlework to keep them from starving.'

Lenin's Last Years

By 1921 Russia had been torn by war, civil war and revolution for seven years. Twenty-eight million people died; many from the fighting but even more from starvation and disease. Nor had the end come to this grisly story. In that year famine swept the Volga region, as a result of a severe drought, and five million died. A year later an American toured south Russia:

'The big trading centre was now a camp crowded with sick and hungry peasants who had fled from their villages, hoping to find food and shelter in the city. Many of them were delirious, some were dying. In a roped-off square I saw uncovered corpses. In the country it was far worse even than in Odessa. There were no doctors in the small communities, no nurses. People moved about the platforms, stepping over prostrate bodies, and the groans of the sick mingled with the never ceasing cry: Khlyeb! Khlyeb! Mi golodni! (Bread! Bread! We're hungry!).'

The chaos and disorder was such that only one-third of the usual crop of grain was harvested. The chief sufferers were the

Collecting the dead during the famine, 1921–22

workers in the towns. The food shortage was made worse by the fact that two-thirds of Russia's locomotives were out of action. Russian industry had almost completely collapsed. Half the workers disappeared; they had either died from fighting, starvation and disease, or they had gone home to the villages in the hope of finding food.

It was not surprising that people blamed the government and its War Communism. Peasants held that the cause of their hardship was the requisitioning bands; in many cases they refused to plant crops except to provide food for their own needs. In the cities the Workers' Opposition grew up. This was made up of trade unionists who complained of the system of workers' books and the muddling of the planners in Moscow, whom they blamed for the collapse of industry. They demanded that control over the management of industries should be given to the unions and taken away from the Communist Party.

Then came 'the flash which lit up reality more than anything else'. The sailors of the naval base on the island of Kronstadt had been in the forefront of the revolutionary movement since 1905. In 1921 they rose once again, this time against the Communist government they had helped to put into power. Now their slogan was 'Soviets without Communists' and they went on to demand free elections, freedom of the press, the sacking of Communist Party men in government jobs and an end to grain requisitioning. The mutiny was put down ruthlessly by Trotsky. Communist troops advanced across the ice which still covered the water surrounding the island. Behind were the Cheka machine gunners to prevent any faint-heartedness. After days of hard fighting the sailors were overcome, but not before thousands of them lay dead in the streets of Kronstadt.

After this, it was clear to Lenin that War Communism had to end if the Communists were to stay in power. It is necessary, he argued, to build 'new gangways to Socialism'. These new gangways were the New Economic Policy.

The NEP

The New Economic Policy, or NEP, was a return to a system of private ownership and private trading. True, Lenin insisted that the government keep control of the 'commanding heights' —banking, power supplies and the very large industries. But

89

A mourner at Lenin's funeral. Notice the ice on this textile worker's mouth

the smaller industries were returned to their private owners,
if they could be found, or to co-operative groups of workers.

The peasants had to pay part of their crops in tax, but any
surplus they grew could be sold privately for their own benefit.
Nearly all buying and selling was done by private traders.
Some of these 'Nepmen' became very rich as they seized the

chance in a time of shortage to buy scarce goods and sell them at a profit.

It took some years for NEP to show its full success, but by 1926 or 1927 it seemed that the country had recovered from the misery and disorder of war. Men might have been tempted to say that normal times had come again. But for most Russians in the middle 'twenties there was still anxiety and doubt.

In January 1924 Vladimir Lenin had died, after being ill for more than a year. He had died before his country had fully recovered from the chaos of the revolution that he dreamed of for twenty years and which, without his leadership, his harshness and his determination would never have survived the first months of opposition. He was truly the founder of Soviet Russia.

8 Stalin

The Struggle for Power
In 1924 the best known Communist leader in Russia was Leon
Trotsky, the hero of the 1905 Soviet, the organizer of the 1917
Revolution and the tireless defender of the government during
the Civil War. Many expected him to take over the leadership
after Lenin and feared this would mean a return to the harsh
days of War Communism, for Trotsky had always stood for
firm control by the Party. Trotsky and his supporters made up
the Left of the Party. On the Right stood the men who had
welcomed the New Economic Policy and the slackening of
strict control by the government and the Party.

This was the great division between the leaders of the
Communist Party in the period after Lenin's death. In the next
few years both Right and Left were destroyed by the man who
had been described by Trotsky as 'the Party's most eminent
mediocrity' and of whom another man wrote, 'He produced,
and not only on me, the impression of a grey blur, looming up
now and then dimly and not leaving any trace. There is really
nothing more to be said about him.'

How did this grey and unknown figure emerge as the ruler of
Russia? Stalin was a plodder, a man to whom ideas never came
in a flash. He was shy and tried to make up for this by rudeness;
he could never rise to power by the brilliance of his speeches or
his writing.

Yet there had always been work for the man who had
changed his opinions rather than quarrel with Lenin and who
would take on dull and tedious jobs. In 1922 Lenin had agreed
to Stalin becoming General Secretary of the Communist
Party, in charge of the Secretariat. Little notice was taken of
this, for no-one saw much importance in the Secretariat. It was
thought that the important bodies in the Party were the Politbureau, which made the vital decisions, and the Central Committee which met only occasionally and usually approved their
leaders' actions.

But the place of the Party in Russian life was growing. There were twice as many party members in 1922 as there had been in 1918. Large numbers of the men in the Party organization, or apparatus, had become full-time officials, not the amateurs who had led the local branches and committees in 1917. They looked to the Secretariat for instructions and they sent in long reports on the problems of their districts. Most of them were appointed to their posts by the Secretariat. So Stalin was in an

Joseph Stalin, photographed in 1950

ideal position to reward his supporters and see that his own ideas were included in instructions sent out to party officials.

He was also in charge of the Control Commission, which was responsible for enquiring into complaints against Party members. Under Stalin, it became the means of carrying out 'purges', expulsions of groups who opposed the Party leadership. In the first year of its work the Control Commission expelled a fifth of the Party membership, most of whom were suspected of being connected with the Workers' Opposition.

It was not long before Lenin saw the dangers of the position he had created for Stalin. When he knew he was dying he wrote a 'Political Will', advising his comrades how to continue after he had gone. He warned them against Stalin: 'Comrade Stalin, having become General Secretary, has concentrated limitless power in his hands, and I am not certain that he will always be careful enough in the use of his power. . . . I propose to the comrades to think over the means of transferring Stalin from this post and appointing to it some other person who is superior to Stalin, in being more tolerant, more loyal, more polite and more attentive to comrades.'

This was read out to the Central Committee after Lenin's death. 'Stalin, who was sitting on the steps of the rostrum, looked small and miserable. I studied him closely; in spite of his self-control and show of calm it was clearly evident that his fate was at stake.' But the situation was saved by Zinoviev, who stood up and said that Stalin's recent behaviour had so much improved that there was no need to carry out Lenin's wishes.

Zinoviev and the other members of the Central Committee had no real love for Stalin. They voted to keep him as General Secretary because they feared Trotsky and believed that, if Stalin and the rest of the Party did not stand together, Trotsky would become a new Russian dictator.

This gave Stalin the time he needed to destroy Trotsky's place in the Party leadership. He did this by encouraging the Right Wing to attack Trotsky. This was a clever move, for many people in Russia looked hopefully to the Right Wing to give them a period of prosperity and freedom from interference. They noted the speeches of Bukharin, the Right Wing leader, who told the peasants 'enrich yourselves'.

Stalin helped the attacks on Trotsky by putting forward a

new slogan, 'Socialism in One Country'. This suggested that the task for Russia was to build up her own agriculture and industry so that she could look forward to a period of peace and stability. Trotsky, on the other hand, was known to believe in 'permanent revolution', which meant a constantly changing society, moving by stages nearer to perfect socialism.

Trotsky was popular in the country and with the troops, but he lacked the determination and ambition to join in a ruthless struggle for power. Perhaps the idea of a ceaseless struggle using underhand methods was distasteful to this man who was a thinker and dreamer by nature. He was also horrified at the idea that he should attack the Party which had done so much for Russia. Most of his attacks on Stalin in the first years after Lenin's death were through writings known only to Party leaders and a few educated Russians. But in 1927 he said that he would work for a change in the government if he thought the country was in danger. He and his followers carried their own banners in the anniversary celebrations of the Bolshevik revolution.

Stalin had been waiting for this moment. 'Enough, comrades', he said, 'an end must be put to this game'. Trotsky was expelled from the Party and exiled to Asiatic Russia. The following year he was deported.

For a brief period of a few months the Right Wing thought they had won a victory, that Russia would settle down and the NEP programme would go on undisturbed. They were soon shaken from this belief. After a serious food shortage, Stalin organized a campaign to seize grain from the rich peasants, using the methods of the War Communism period. When, throughout the country, Communist Party officials tried to object to this sudden change of policy they were purged in their thousands. Bukharin, the leader of the Right, now realized that the real danger of dictatorship lay with Stalin: 'He will strangle us. He is an unprincipled intriguer who subordinates everything to his appetite for power. At any given moment he will change his theories in order to get rid of someone.'

The realization came to Bukharin too late. Before the end of 1929 he had been dismissed from the Politbureau and several supporters, including the Prime Minister, lost their posts. Stalin, the Secretary of the Communist Party, was the master of Russia.

	Last year of peace 1913	End of NEP 1928	Middle of third plan 1940
pig iron	4·2	3·3	15·0 m tons
steel	4·2	4·3	18·3
coal	29·1	35·5	166
oil	9·2	11·7	31
cement	1·5	1·8	5·8
tractors	none	1,200	31,000
motor vehicles	none	700	145,000
grain	81	73	95·5 m tons

The production, each year, of important goods. Note how little progress was made between 1913 and 1928.

The Five Year Plans

Even before his defeat of the Right Opposition, Stalin and his supporters had begun to prepare for the development of Russia into a modern industrialized country. This arose from his belief in 'Socialism in one Country'. Russia had to build herself up to prove to the rest of the world that socialism worked. 'We are fifty or a hundred years behind the advanced countries. We must make good this lag in ten years. Either we do it or they crush us. . . .'

The Party decided that it wanted 'the transformation of our country from an agrarian into an industrial one, capable by its own means of producing the necessary equipment.' But this could not be done by NEP methods, which were really designed to encourage peasants to increase their grain growing. So, in 1928, the NEP was replaced by the first Five Year Plan. This was not a general programme but a law which laid down the rate of increase for industry and agriculture for the five years 1928–32. All the emphasis was on heavy industry and fuel supplies which were essential if Russia was to become an industrial country. Heavy industry was to increase its output by three hundred per cent and six times as much electricity was to be produced. All Russia's efforts had to go into these fields and the industries which produced consumer goods—clothes, furniture and other goods used up or consumed by private citizens—were to develop much more slowly.

A board in Moscow shows the progress of the first Five Year Plan

An astonishing transformation came over Russia in the
1930s as the first, second and third Five Year Plans were carried
out. The table on page 96 shows the increase in the major
industries. It does not show the vast new iron and steel works
that grew up in the Urals, Europe's largest hydro-electric plant
on the River Dnieper, the new tractor works, or the automobile
plants in Moscow and Gorky. In the period of the first Five Year
Plan alone, 1,500 new industrial plants were built. The second
and third Plans stressed transport and resulted in a 100,000

miles of air-line, new motor roads, and waterways such as the
141 miles Baltic–White Sea Canal. Old towns were enlarged
and new ones sprang up. Stalinsk, the centre of a new coal
producing region, grew from a village of 4,000 people to a city
of 170,000 by 1939.

Just before the Second World War broke out, Russia had
increased her industrial output by four hundred per cent from
the beginning of World War One. In many other countries
production in this period had actually fallen. But the cost to
the Russian people had been terrible, and the Five Year Plans
had been fulfilled only by the harshest measures.

In theory, the workers had been consulted about the planning of their factory's work, but in practice this was always done
by Gosplan, the State Planning Committee in Moscow which
laid down very detailed programmes for each industry.
Workers' meetings called to approve the plans were packed
with Communist Party members, who made speeches in favour
of the target they had been set and voted to support it. The
hardships of the workers increased greatly as the planners put
more and more demands on them. The workers' book system
of the War Communism period was brought back. No worker
could be employed without it and he had to hand it over to
each new employer, who would inspect it for endorsements
showing the 'crimes' of lateness, absenteeism and bad work-
manship. Hours of work were increased, but many workers'
wages went down because most of them were paid on piece-
rates fixed according to the production of the most skilled and
strongest.

The best workers were publicly honoured as part of propaganda campaigns to encourage the hard-driven Russians to
even greater efforts. In 1935 Alexis Stakhanov succeeded in
producing 102 tons of coal in a six-hour shift. For this feat he
was made a hero and the figure-head of the Stakhanovite
movement. Stakhanovite workers were given extra pay, free
holidays and visits to the Kremlin to receive their award of the
Order of Lenin and the title Hero of Socialist Labour which
went with it.

But for every Stakhanovite there were hundreds of workers
whose pay fell and whose strength wasted away. They were
driven on by Party officials, who continually raised the targets

Woman at work in the tractor factory in Stalingrad

for production and who invented new campaigns and 'drives'
for special efforts.

There was no relief from misery and hardship outside the
factory. Food and goods of every kind were rationed and
scarcer than they had been before the Five Year Plans began.
There was a terrible shortage of housing, particularly in the
new towns where workers lived in tents and barracks.

An OGPU[1] agent reported angry criticism of the Party at a
factory meeting:

'You well-fed devils have sucked the juices out of us enough.

[1] OGPU was the new name for the Cheka, or secret police.

For twelve years you have drivelled and agitated and stuffed our heads . . . the factory owners did not force us to work in four shifts and there was enough of everything in the shops. Now we work in four shifts. . . . If you go to a shop now and want to buy something the shops are empty.'

It soon became dangerous to make such criticisms. The OGPU were constantly looking for people to bring to trial for 'sabotage', although usually the real crime was to have criticized the Party. The trials were stage-managed and everyone knew the prisoners would be found guilty. Their real purpose was to frighten others who might be tempted to criticize the Party. An American watched a prosecutor make a ten-hour summing up of the 'case' against a group of fifty-one engineers: 'he had reached a state of frenzy where he spat words of venom, hurling them at his victims in a fit of raving madness. As if carried away by a lust for murder, he demanded death for every defendant, punctuating each demand with the shriek: "*Razstryel!*" (Shooting!) and smacking his lips.'

Perhaps the prisoners who were shot were the lucky ones. For the rest the sentence was likely to be forced labour. This was the means of finding the workers needed for the hardest tasks. Three hundred thousand worked to cut the Baltic–White Sea canal; others struggled in the coal mines, in forestry works and on railways in Siberia and the Far North. The Ministry of the Interior, which organized these schemes, had no fewer than ten million workers, most of whom died before their term was completed.

Collectivization

If Russia was to industrialize she needed money, raw materials and workers. In a country which was almost entirely agricultural, the only place where these could come from was the countryside. To provide the money to invest in industry the only people who could be taxed were the peasants; to feed the growing numbers of workers in the towns cheap food was necessary; to carry out the work large numbers of peasants had to be moved from the countryside to the towns. To Stalin, all these needs of the Five Year Plan pointed to one inescapable answer; the peasants must give up their private farms and join

collectives. Collectives were to be village farms run by a committee, which would organize the farming and sell the produce
after the state had taken its share in taxation. The committees
would be controlled by Communists who would drive the
peasants to produce what the state needed in food and raw
materials and drive unwanted peasants away to work in the
towns. Peasants were to be paid according to the number of
work-days they gave to the collective. All their live-stock and
equipment would be handed over for the use of the collective
as a whole.

A typical peasant woman of the 1930s

Stalin believed that collectivization would come about peacefully, but there were very few peasants who wished to give up farms which had only been theirs since the revolution. He claimed that it was only the Kulaks, the rich peasants, who opposed collectivization and tried to whip up the feelings of the poor peasants against them. 'We must liquidate the Kulaks as a class', he said. But in fact, nearly all were against collectivization and the campaign against the Kulaks became an attack on the whole peasantry. Even peasant leaders of many village soviets joined in the resistance.

In 1929, police and army units went into the countryside to 'liquidate the Kulaks'. In most places there was fierce resistance and collectivization was only carried out after villages had been surrounded by machine-gunners. An English visitor met a colonel of the OGPU: 'I'm an old Bolshevik,' he said, almost sobbing. 'I worked in the underground against the Tsar and then I fought in the civil war. Did I do all that in order that I should now surround villages with machine-guns and order my men to fire indiscriminately into crowds of peasants? Oh, no, no!'

Hundreds of thousands had their property confiscated and were deported into Siberia or labour camps. But these were not the only ones to resent collectivization. In a great wave of anger, millions of Russian peasants burned crops and killed their livestock. They hid their grain after the harvest. In 1934 Stalin reported sadly that the number of cattle and horses had been halved since 1928 and that pigs, sheep and goats had dropped by one third. Part of the loss was due to bad harvests followed by terrible famines in the Ukraine.

This was one reason for the hardship in the towns under the Five Year Plans. Another was the poor quality of the farming. Many peasants had only ever used wooden ploughs; they were unused to chemical fertilizers and knew little about the proper care of animals. The government tried to improve this by the work of the Mechanical and Tractor Stations (MTS) which were set up throughout the countryside. The plan was that these should loan tractors and mechanical equipment to the collectives and give them advice on improving their farming. But there was a chronic shortage of equipment; there were only 7,000 tractors in the whole of Russia in 1929 and, even in 1939,

Threshing on a collective farm

The cotton crop from a collective in Asiatic Russia

many collectives never had the use of one. The MTS's were also unable to concentrate on giving advice and help because the government used them as propaganda and police centres. The deputy director was always a member of the OGPU and this fact made peasants much less willing to seek advice from the MTS.

Stalin's policy was a failure; he lost the support of the peasants and he failed to encourage them to produce the food he needed. In 1939 food production was just creeping up to the 1928 level, but in the meantime the Russian population had grown from about 150 million to about 170 million.

The Great Purges

Stalin dismayed many Russians by the fierceness and cruelty he used to get collectivization and the Five Year Plans under way. But, in the early 'thirties, his terrorist methods were not used against Party members. Even the arch enemy, Trotsky, had been allowed to escape with his life. The victims of the many purges of the Communist Party had lost their privileges as Party members, and in many cases their jobs, but very few had been persecuted any further.

Perhaps this was because Stalin knew the dangers of attacking his colleagues. 'You chop off one head today, another one tomorrow, still another the day after—what in the end will be left of the party?' It certainly was not because he was afraid of bloodshed. Lady Astor asked him in 1931, 'How long are you going to kill people?'

'As long as it is necessary', Stalin replied.

But there must have been many among the leaders of the Communist Party who thought that the shooting of Kulaks and suspected saboteurs went much too far. Even Yagoda, the OGPU chief, sometimes reduced sentences which had been passed on Stalin's orders. By the middle of the 1930s these Communists' distrust of Stalin had grown very bitter. Many of them were 'Old Bolsheviks', who had joined the revolution before 1917 and who had never imagined that they would end up at the head of a state which was every bit as brutal as the old Tsarist empire. Stalin's impatience with them grew year by year, particularly when he found that many younger Communists agreed with their dislike of his methods.

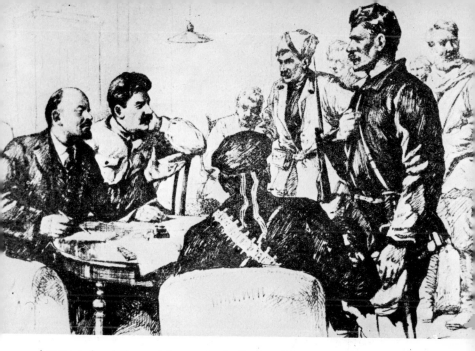

A propaganda painting made in 1937 showing Lenin and Stalin together in 1917.
Stalin ordered many such paintings to give the impression that he had been Lenin's
close companion at the time of the revolution. This was untrue

Stalin may have been jealous of some of his comrades. He
was a dull man whose writings and speeches were utterly
boring, compared with those of other members of the Politbureau. He was jealous of the popularity of the other leaders
like Kirov, the head of the Leningrad Party organization, who
had no difficulty in being on good terms with everybody.

Stalin's personal life had been unhappy. In 1932 his wife
committed suicide, following a Stalinist purge of the Communist
Party in the Moscow Technical Institute where she was a
student. Whatever the reason, he began in 1935 a most terrible
blood-letting which resulted in hundreds of thousands of
deaths.

It started with the murder of Kirov in December 1934. Stalin
had a hand in this and in the faked car accident in which the
only witness died shortly after. Immediately the OGPU was
ordered to speed up its investigation of cases of 'terrorism'.
This was, in fact, an instruction to round up and put on trial
anti-Stalinist Communists. The ground was prepared well in
Moscow and Leningrad by the appointment of two new young

New Hydro-electric station at Tashkent, 1931

The Moscow Underground, a show-piece of Stalin's Russia. Notice the marble pillars. The underground was built at great speed and under dangerous conditions. Much of the work was done by political prisoners

Stalinists as heads of the Communist Parties in the two great cities. In Leningrad, Zhdanov carried out a purge of tens of thousands of Kirov supporters who were soon on their way to Siberian labour camps. In Moscow, Nikita Khrushchev became Party Secretary. He was soon screaming in Red Square after a trial of 'Trotskyites': 'The working people of Moscow . . . fervently approve the fair sentence on the enemies of the people, the foul gang of pre-revolutionary Trotskyites. We draw our proletarian sword to chop off the heads of the loathsome creatures, double-dealers and murderers, agents of fascism. The mad beast must be finished off.'

With such reliable henchmen in key positions, Stalin set up the great show trials of 1936 and 1937. Into the dock in Moscow stepped all the great names of the 1920s; the whole of Lenin's Politbureau except Trotsky and Stalin himself were there. So were the chiefs of the Red Army and the Soviet Navy. Even Yagoda, the OGPU chief, appeared. More incredible were the confessions. These national heroes solemnly agreed that they had plotted with foreign nations to overthrow the Russian government or to kill Lenin and Stalin. The confessions had, of course, been extracted by torture on men wearied by long months of solitary confinement. When one retracted his confession, the court sitting was promptly adjourned by the prosecutor who had no real evidence prepared. The next day Vyshinsky was back demanding as usual, 'Shoot the mad dogs.'

After the figureheads had been taken away and shot it was the turn of the lesser members of the Party. One-fifth of all the officers in the Red Army were liquidated. Every local Communist Party was purged of 'Trotskyites'. Khrushchev was one of many Party officials loyal to Stalin sent to carry out this bloody work in the countryside. In 1938 he was made First Secretary of the Ukraine Communist Party with instructions 'to deal the final blow at all this Trotskyite, Bukharinite and bourgeois nationalist gang in the Ukraine.'

In 1939 Stalin called a halt to the terror. But the work had been thoroughly done. The Politbureau was now made up entirely of Stalin's men—Molotov, Khrushchev, Zhdanov and Beria, the new chief of the secret police (now renamed the NKVD). Half a million Party members had been promoted to

E

new positions in the previous five years, most of them new Communists replacing purged and liquidated Old Bolsheviks.

There was a postscript to the Great Purge. Since his exile, Trotsky had carried out a bitter paper war against Stalin. In books and in his paper, the *Bulletin of the Opposition*, which was widely but secretly read in Russia, he had attacked Stalin for his inhuman policies and for his new dictatorship. In 1940 he was in Mexico, having already escaped several attempts at assassination by Stalin's agents. On 20 August, while he was writing a life of Stalin, he was killed by a blow to the head with an ice-axe. Stalin had succeeded in eliminating his greatest rival at last.

9 Russia at Peace and War 1917–1945

The Comintern

Lenin and Trotsky had spent so many years in exile that they had as many friends—as well as enemies—among socialists in other countries as they had in Russia. They had always seen communism as an international movement and expected widespread proletarian revolution to break out once they had established a base in Russia. After World War One there were three revolutions, one in Hungary and two in Germany, but they were easily crushed by the governments of these countries. This disappointed Lenin, who hoped that a European-wide revolutionary movement would force the governments to withdraw the troops that were helping the Whites in the Civil War.

The great weakness that Lenin saw in the European socialist movement was in the leadership of the Second International. This body had been set up in 1889 to act as a joint organization of all social democratic parties. By the end of World War One most of these parties had split. The largest groups, such as the English Labour Party, had ceased to be revolutionary and worked to win power through elections.

In 1919 Lenin called a meeting of the revolutionary socialists in Moscow to set up a Third International. This became known as the Communist International, or Comintern, and the groups which accepted its leadership split away from the Social Democratic or Labour Parties and renamed themselves Communists.

From the earliest days, the Comintern met in Moscow and the Russian Communist Party always took the lead in deciding its activities. The other Communist parties were willing to follow the instructions of the Russians who were, after all, the only Communists who had been successful revolutionaries. There was little opportunity for revolution in Europe, however, and much of the work of Comintern agents was in trying to build up communist parties in the poor countries of Asia and South America. In Europe their main activity was to organize political campaigns and demonstrations.

Stalin and Germany

Stalin had rarely been outside Russia and knew little of the European socialist movement. His belief in 'Socialism in one country' meant that he saw the defence of the Soviet Union as more important than spreading revolution, and his main object in the 1920s and 1930s was to keep Russia out of another war. Like most other statesmen he thought the greatest threat to peace would come from Germany.

At the Peace Conference at Versailles in 1919, the western allies had decided that Germany must be so weakened that she would never again rise to be a world power. Territories were taken from her eastern and western borders, a large part of her industrial plant and railway stock was seized and she was presented with a fantastic bill for reparations—payments for the cost of the war. But Germany was not the only nation to be humiliated at Versailles. The allies had refused to allow Communist Russia to take part in the conference. At that time no state would officially recognize the Communists as the legal government of Russia and all trading relations with her were broken off.

It was natural that the two outcast nations should draw together. On Easter Sunday, 1922, they signed the Treaty of Rapallo, by which Germany became the first country to give Russia full recognition and both countries agreed to exchange trade and military advice. At the end of the 1920s Hitler began the last stages of his rise to power. Stalin under-estimated the danger. At this time when it was vitally important that all opponents of nazism should stand together, the Cominterm advised German Communists to oppose German Socialists in elections. There were bitter struggles between Communists and Socialists for power in German trade unions. This weakened the Socialist Party, the largest in the German parliament with the best chance of resisting Hitler. When Hitler became Chancellor in 1933 Stalin saw his mistake. The Communist Party in Germany was banned and persecuted. Worse, Hitler was clearly planning a drive to the east, through the states which separated Germany from Russia.

When he realized the danger, Stalin changed his policy and tried to establish good relations with other powers. Russia joined the League of Nations in 1934. Ministers from many countries were welcomed in Russia. The Comintern was told to campaign for 'popular fronts' in which Communists would co-operate with Liberals and Socialists to bring about governments which would oppose the spread of fascism. But the Popular Front movements were suspected of being Russian led and Russia was especially feared because this was the time of the Great Purge.

Britain and France were not sure if the Red Army could ever recover from the execution of so many of its officers. At the same time Stalin doubted whether the Western Powers would stand up to Hitler. They had not resisted in 1936 when his troops re-occupied the Rhineland, which had been taken from Germany in 1919. Britain refused to help the Republican government in Spain when it was attacked by the fascist forces of General Franco, who was aided by arms from Hitler and Mussolini. Hitler's intentions in eastern Europe were becoming menacingly clear. In 1938 Austria was forced to unite with Germany. A few months later came the Munich agreement, in which the British Prime Minister accepted Hitler's word that he would take no more territory once he had been given part of Czechoslovakia. Stalin knew eastern Europe better and forecast that Hitler would soon seize the rest of Czechoslovakia and then Poland.

So, while continuing to press for an understanding with Britain and France, Stalin began to re-open the door to friend-

Ribbentrop flies to Moscow, August 1939

ship with Germany. Throughout 1939 the double game went on until, in August, he decided that the only way to save Russia was to sign a treaty with Hitler.

On 23 August 1939, Ribbentrop, the German Foreign Minister, flew to Moscow. After a day of talks with Molotov, the Russian Foreign Minister, the Russo-German Pact was signed. Each power agreed not to attack the other if she was involved in a war with another state. This meant that, for a time at least, Stalin need not fear a German invasion. Hitler knew that if he marched into Poland Russia would not come to her defence. A week later his armies invaded Poland. Britain and France had previously agreed to declare war if this happened and, on 3 September 1939, World War Two began.

September 1939 to June 1941

The Molotov–Ribbentrop agreement contained secret clauses. Germany agreed that she would not stand in Russia's way if she occupied eastern Poland, the Baltic states of Latvia and Estonia, and Finland. After the German attack on Poland the Russian armies moved forward into these areas. Only the Finns put up strong resistance until they were forced to hand over the parts of their country nearest to Russia in March, 1940.

In Poland the Germans persecuted the Jews while the Russians imprisoned and executed Poles suspected of being anti-Communist. Fifteen thousand Polish officers were taken to the Soviet Union, never to be heard of again. Later in the war the Germans claimed they had found a mass grave with thousands of their bodies.

The occupation of these lands gave Stalin the feeling that Russia was now secure against German attack and, throughout 1940, relations were friendly. Russia traded with Germany and allowed Hitler's warships to use her naval bases. The Comintern instructed all Communists in the allied countries to oppose the war against Germany.

In 1941 relations worsened. After the fall of France in 1940, Hitler calculated that he could afford to swing his armies into an attack on Russia. The alliance was weakened by the breakdown of talks between Molotov and Ribbentrop in Berlin. The Germans had proposed that Russia stand by while they occupied Roumania and Bulgaria. Molotov firmly insisted that

SCALE OF MILES

0 50 100 150 200

Territory annexed by Germany
September 1939

Territory annexed by U.S.S.R.
September 1939

SWEDEN

ESTONIA

U.

BALTIC SEA

Riga
LATVIA

S.

Memel
LITHUANIA

Danzig

EAST
PRUSSIA

Minsk

G
Berlin

Oder

Vistula

Poznan

Warsaw
Brest-Litovsk

S.

E

P O L A N D

R

Neisse

Oder

Lodz

Lublin

Bug

M

A
Prague

C Z E C H O -

R.

N

S L O V A K I A

Stanislav

Y
Vienna

Poland divided between Russia and Germany, September 1939

these two countries must remain in the Russian sphere of interest. He was also a little sarcastic and pointed out that England might not agree. 'England', said Ribbentrop, 'is finished. She is no more use as a power.' 'If that is so,' Molotov replied, 'why are we in this shelter and whose bombs are falling?'

The following month Hitler called his military staff together and gave orders for Operation Barbarossa: 'the German Armed Forces must be prepared to crush Soviet Russia even before the conclusion of war against England.'

The Great Fatherland War

Despite the bad relations between the two countries in 1941, Stalin did not expect an attack and had refused to believe warnings of German preparations passed on to him by the British Secret Service. So nothing was done to prepare the Russian armies or the Russian people for the sudden swoop made by the Germans on 22 June at many different places on the 1,800 mile western frontier of Russia.

The speed and success of the first German moves seemed to prove that Hitler had been right when he told his generals: 'We have only to kick in the door and the whole rotten structure will come crashing down.' In the first fortnight the Russians lost a million men, nearly the whole of their air-force and thousands of tanks. They had been ill-prepared. The pilots had rarely done more than 15 hours' solo flying time, most tank-drivers had only practised for one-and-a-half or two hours. More important, the Red Army was not prepared for the *blitzkrieg*, the massive attack by a rapidly moving motorized army. Many Russian guns were drawn by horses; there were still officers who preferred the telephone to the wireless set.

By October the three main German armies had reached the end of their first thrusts. The Northern Army Group was shelling Leningrad, the Central Group was within sight of Moscow, and the Southern Army had overrun most of the Crimea and was on its way to the oil-fields of Caucasia. Behind them lay a vast area of occupied territory containing eighty million people, most of whom were to suffer terribly during the next two years. Many at first welcomed the Germans as an army of liberation from the Communist dictatorship. But the behaviour of the invaders soon lost them this support. Western Russia was ear-marked as the land which was to make up Germany's shortage of food and labour. Three million young workers were deported to Germany, leaving behind the elderly, who struggled to grow food to meet the greedy demands of their new masters. The Jews were persecuted viciously, particularly at the village

Russians look at their homes destroyed by the Germans, 1942

of Babyi Yar where 100,000 were massacred.

Stalin was badly shaken by the success of the first German attacks, but he recovered and began to give tireless energy to the task of driving out the invaders. He broadcast to the Russian people: 'The Red Army and Navy and the whole Soviet people must fight for every inch of Soviet soil, fight to the last drop of our blood for our towns and villages. We must organize every kind of help for the Red Army, make sure that its ranks are constantly renewed and that it is supplied with everything it needs.'

The first task was to save Russian industry from the invader. In a massive effort, about 1,500 factories were moved away from Leningrad and the western frontier lands to the safety of the Urals and Siberia. Altogether there were one-and-a-half million wagon loads. Following them came the workers, who spent the cruel winter of 1941–42 rebuilding their factories and re-assembling their machinery, working fifteen hours a day so that production should be delayed as little as possible.

The greatest need was to keep up the spirits and courage of

the Russian people and to prevent panic. Stalin set a lead here by refusing to leave the Kremlin when the Germans advanced on Moscow. He tried to show himself not, as he had been in the 1930s, the boss of a Communist state, but as a national hero leading the whole Russian people. In his speeches he referred to the great heroes of Tsarist days. He often reminded the Russians of 1812, when Napoleon had invaded and they had suffered terrible hardship before the French were driven out. That was the first Fatherland War; the struggle against Germany was named the Second Fatherland War. A fierce hatred of the Germans was whipped up. A famous Russian writer said: 'We must not say, "Good morning" or "Goodnight". In the morning we must say, "Kill the Germans", and at night we must say, "Kill the Germans". We want to live and in order to live, we must kill Germans.'

All this was necessary because the Russian people suffered terribly. Rations were low, and housing and fuel shortages brought widespread sickness which resulted in fifteen million early deaths by the end of the war. Women were drafted for work in factories, holidays were abolished and the average working week was seventy-seven hours.

To strengthen further the sense that the Russians were fighting for their own land and traditions, Stalin lifted the ban which had been placed on the Russian Orthodox Church at the Revolution. He also took steps to end some of the grievances of the army officers. The Political Commissars were made the subordinates of the officers, not their masters as they had been in the Civil War. Special badges of rank for army officers were brought back.

These measures were undertaken hastily because of the desperate state of the war. In the spring of 1942 the enemy was preparing for the final attack on Moscow and Leningrad.

LENINGRAD

Leningrad's position was by far the worst. The city was almost completely surrounded by German forces and the only possible supply route was across Lake Ladoga. The barges which crossed in summer, and the lorries which drove across the ice in winter, were continually bombed by German aircraft. The result was starvation:

'To fill their empty stomachs, to reduce the intense sufferings caused by hunger, people would look for incredible substitutes: they would try to catch crows and rooks, or any cat or dog that had somehow survived; they would go through medicine chests in search of castor oil, hair oil, vaseline or glycerine; they would make soup or jelly out of carpenter's glue.'

Despite such measures, at least two-thirds of a million people died during the siege. Leningrad was saved by the men and women who volunteered to fight in front of the city and those who worked furiously under continual bombardment to manufacture shells. It was not until January 1944 that relief came and the Germans were driven away by Russian armies that could at last be spared from the fighting further south.

MOSCOW

As the Germans advanced on Moscow, the city prepared to defend itself. Communist brigades were formed from among the workers, both men and women, and taken out to the front to meet the oncoming Germans. A young woman weaver described her part in the defence of the city:

'I was ordered, like most of the girls at the factory, to join the Labour Front. We were taken some kilometres out of Moscow. There was a large crowd of us, and we were told to dig trenches. We were all very calm, but dazed and couldn't take it. On the very first day we were machine-gunned by a Fritz who swooped right down. Eleven of the girls were killed and four wounded.'

The Moscow people played a big part in holding up the Germans. In December 1941 another ally came to help the Red Army. This was 'General Winter', the long bitter Russian winter when the frozen ground was covered by several feet of snow. The Russians knew what to expect, but Hitler had not prepared his armies for winter fighting. Their boots were tight fitting and had iron nails which conducted the heat away. The Russians wore loose, nail-less boots which they padded with paper and old clothing. Two days after Hitler stopped the advance of his armies until the spring, Stalin ordered the Russian counter-attack. Slowly and wearily the German armies were pushed two or three hundred miles to the west. After this the Russian armies were too exhausted to continue. But the

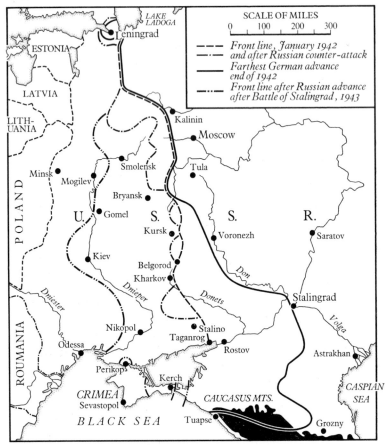

SCALE OF MILES

0   100   200   300

– – – *Front line, January 1942*
–·– *and after Russian counter-attack*
—— *Farthest German advance*
         end of 1942
–··– *Front line after Russian advance*
         after Battle of Stalingrad, 1943

The War in Russia

counter-attack saved Moscow, and the German armies did not return. Leningrad was still besieged but the main weight of the next German attack, in the spring of 1942, was turned south towards the Caucasus.

STALINGRAD

The German advance in the south in 1942 was as strong and rapid as the invasion in 1941. Then they were held up at Stalingrad—the city of Stalin—on the Volga. Hitler need not have fought there; he could have by-passed the town with the main part of his army, but he was determined to capture the city which bore the name of his great rival. The battle of Stalingrad became one of the most decisive in World War Two. Hitler starved his other battle-fronts of troops so that he could pour a third of a million men and much of his best equipment into the struggle.

Stalin was equally determined. 'I demand of you every measure to defend Stalingrad. Stalingrad must not be yielded to the enemy', he ordered, when already the defending troops had been cut off from the main Red Army. The workers of Stalingrad joined them and for two months, hand to hand fighting for single factories and houses held up the Germans. Then, as he had done at Moscow the year before, Stalin ordered a counter-attack when winter fell. The Red Army swept round the Germans and trapped them in the 'Stalingrad cauldron', where it was their turn to suffer the terrors of being in a besieged city in winter with no food supplies. Hitler refused to allow the German general to fight his way back to the west. He left his army in Stalingrad to be steadily cut to pieces until, in February 1943, the few surviving units surrendered. Stalingrad cost Hitler 300,000 of Germany's best troops.

'The Russians', said Winston Churchill, 'tore the guts out of the German army'. The part they played in drawing in the cream of Hitler's forces and then destroying them made it certain that the Allies would eventually win World War Two. Ernest Bevin, a Labour leader, summed up Britain's gratitude to the Russians: 'All the aid we have been able to give has been small compared with the tremendous efforts of the Soviet people. Our children's children will look back through their history books, with admiration and thanks for the heroism of the great Russian people.'

1943 to 1945

The Stalingrad defeat meant that Hitler had to withdraw his troops from South Russia. The war had reached its turning point. Before the end of 1943 the Germans were in retreat along the whole front, except at Leningrad where they were not driven away until the spring of 1944.

When the time came to launch the main campaign of 1944, the armaments factories in the Urals were producing a stream of arms and ammunition for the Red Army. Allied aid had been

flowing for the past two years and Stalin had 400,000 Stude-
baker trucks from America to transport his men. 'The Red
Army', he announced, 'has become the most powerful and
steeled of modern armies.'

Victory over Germany was certain; so Stalin's main concern
was to make sure that, after the War, Russia would be safe-
guarded against the invasions she had suffered in 1914 and
1941. His first goal was to keep the lands that he had gained
from the Pact with the Germans in 1939: Latvia, Estonia,
Lithuania and Eastern Poland. But he was also determined
that the other states of eastern Europe should fall under Soviet
influence.

Between 1943 and 1945 the three major allies, Russia,
America and Britain, argued out their plans for the post-war
world. Stalin, Roosevelt and Churchill met together at Teheran
in Persia in 1943. Roosevelt was anxious to please Stalin but
Churchill was suspicious of his aims in Europe. In 1944 Russia
and Britain agreed to divide the Balkans into spheres of influence. Russia was to have the chief voice in establishing governments in Bulgaria, Roumania and Hungary, leaving Greece to

The 'big three' at Teheran, 1943

Britain, whose forces were already fighting the Germans there. The two powers were to share influence in Yugoslavia.

The outstanding question was then Poland. Refugee Polish politicians had set up a government-in-exile in London which was hostile to the Russians. It expected the British to demand that Russia should retire from eastern Poland and recognize them as the true government of Poland. The British wished to back the government-in-exile, but could see no way of preventing Stalin doing as he wanted with lands so close to his frontier. A compromise was reached in 1945 when the 'big three' met again at Yalta in the Crimea. Roosevelt and Churchill agreed that Poland should give up her eastern lands to Russia and in return take some territory from eastern Germany. Stalin promised that some non-Communists would be allowed to serve in the Polish government.

At Yalta, the three powers also agreed that, after the war, Germany should be divided into four zones, occupied by troops from Russia, America, Britain and France. They then went on to make the arrangements for establishing the United Nations, as a means of preserving peace in the post-war world.

The End of the War

The allies agreed that Hitler must be forced to make an unconditional surrender. They refused to make any bargain which would leave him in power in return for an early ending to the war. This meant that their armies would have to fight their way across Europe to Berlin. The invasion of German occupied lands began in 1944.

In the west the Americans and British landed troops in Normandy; in the east the Red Army entered Roumania, Bulgaria and Yugoslavia, driving the Germans before them. It was not long before the governments which had collaborated with the Germans were overthrown and new coalition governments set up.

In the same year, 1944, the Red Army entered Poland. It had already formed a Polish government, the so-called Lublin committee, composed of Communists and their supporters. In doing this it had ignored the Polish government-in-exile in London.

Stalin was master of the Polish situation and the Red Army

Warsaw after the rising against the Germans

was the only force which could control events there. This was made clear in September 1944. As the Russian armies approached Poland's capital, Warsaw, its people rose in rebellion against the Germans. The Germans turned on them and put down the revolt with great savagery, dismantling Warsaw almost brick by brick. The Russians were unable to advance quickly enough to save the Poles; yet they refused to allow British and American planes to use Soviet airstrips to fly in supplies which might have made it possible for the Polish Resistance to hold out. The Poles claimed that the Russians had deliberately allowed the Warsaw resistance to be destroyed because its members supported the government-in-exile.

In 1945 the Russian armies rolled on through Czechoslovakia, Hungary and Germany. They closed in on Berlin where, on 30 April, Hitler killed himself in his underground headquarters. On 8 May the German army surrendered to the British and on 9 May to the Russians.

10 The Cold War

Eastern Europe after the War
When Stalin had agreed with Britain about the division of Russian and British influence in eastern Europe he had no carefully worked-out plans for the states which were to fall under Russian influence. All he had asked was that they should have governments friendly to Russia, who would have the right to ban fascist politicians. It was quite reasonable that Russia should wish to safeguard her interests in this way. Of all the eastern European governments occupied by the Russians only one, Czechoslovakia, had had a democratic government before the war. Part of Hitler's success had certainly been due to the friendship of the petty dictators of eastern Europe.

The wartime resistance to the Germans had usually been split between two groups, one receiving help and advice from London, and a Communist movement keeping in close contact with Moscow. During the war, Stalin had held regular conferences for the leaders of the Communist parties in eastern Europe. These had been concerned both with fighting the Germans and with making preparations for the period after the war.

As the Russians occupied the various Eastern European countries, they set up coalition governments which usually had Communists in the Ministry of the Interior, controlling the police, in the Army and in the broadcasting services. Thus, in every country in which Britain agreed to Russia having the main interest and in two others (Czechoslovakia and the tiny Albania), Stalin had got the anti-fascist government he had asked for at Yalta.

During the next two years the friendliness between Russia and America began to break down. One reason for this was the death of President Roosevelt, who had been sympathetic to Stalin's search for secure frontiers. His successor, President Truman, was suspicious of Russia and believed that it was necessary to show toughness to her. He wrote: 'Unless Russia is faced with an iron fist and strong language, another war is in

SCALE OF MILES
0 100 200 300 400 500

▮ Lands gained by U.S.S.R.
from her Western neighbours
▨ Members of the Communist bloc

Europe after the War

the making. Only one language do they understand—"how
many divisions have you?"'

Truman decided not to let Russia into the secrets of the
Atomic Bomb, which was first used in a raid on Japan in
August 1945. Stalin, for his part, disturbed the western powers
by interfering in the governments of Roumania and Bulgaria,
and by the Russian management of their zone in Germany.
They dismantled large sections of German industry which were
taken to Russia in payment for war damages and refused to
allow food to be moved from their sector in the east, where

most of it was grown, to the western sectors. A large number of Communists were placed in the government of East Germany.

These disagreements in 1945 to 1947 taught the world two new phrases: 'iron curtain' and 'cold war'. Winston Churchill, speaking at Fulton in the USA, drew attention to the iron curtain dividing eastern Europe from the rest of the world:

'From Stettin in the Baltic to Trieste in the Adriatic, an iron curtain has descended across the Continent. Behind that curtain lie all the capitals of the ancient states of central and eastern Europe . . . and all are subject, in one form or another, not only to Soviet influence but to a very high and in some cases increasing measure of control from Moscow.'

The Cold War

The Cold War became an obvious part of the international scene in 1947. In March President Truman announced the Truman Doctrine, declaring that America would give military and economic help to any country which was threatened by Russia. A few months later, through the Marshall Plan, the Americans offered to give economic help to European countries including Russia and her satellites. Russia refused help for herself and would not allow the satellites to take Marshall Aid, on the grounds that it was nothing but a trick to bring them under American influence.

Stalin began to tighten his control over the eastern European countries. Gradually the power of the Communists in their governments was increased and other parties and their leaders driven out of office and into prison. Hungary, Roumania, Bulgaria and Poland, all became People's Democracies, as Yugoslavia had in 1945. They were closely modelled on the Soviet Union, which meant that the communist parties were the real governments. Each country had to accept a large number of Soviet advisers who directed them to develop their countries in the way that Russia indicated. Farms were collectivized and industries nationalized. The communist parties were purged in the same way as the Russian party. Most serious was the Russian control of the economic life of these countries. They were forced to produce the goods most wanted by Russia and sell them to her at extremely low prices. The

Poles sold coal to Russia at one-tenth of the price offered by Denmark.

In 1947 the Communist Information Bureau, or Cominform, was set up, to co-ordinate the propaganda of the Soviet bloc and the communist parties of France and Italy where communism was strong. The Cominform created 'front organizations' such as the Peace Committees set up in most European countries to campaign against American policies. The American Central Intelligence Agency was equally active, with radio stations beaming propaganda and secret financing of anti-Communist journals.

In 1948, the Cold War centred on Berlin. The German capital lay in the Eastern Zone but was divided into four sectors. After the Russians announced their plans for turning East Germany into a People's Democracy, the western powers united their zones with a view to establishing a West German government. The Russians then closed the railways and roads from the Western Zone to Berlin, which meant that food supplies for West Berlin were cut off. Britain, France and America supplied the West Berliners by the 'Berlin Airlift' for nearly a year before Stalin broke off the blockade.

In 1949 the Cold War reached a stalemate in Europe. On the one side stood the Soviet bloc, closely controlled by Moscow and occupied by about two million Red Army soldiers. On the other, the Americans and their European allies set up the North Atlantic Treaty Organization. The main part of NATO's forces was American. They had the advantage of a stock of nuclear weapons, whereas the Soviet Union only tested her first atomic bomb in 1949.

Another gain for the west was the quarrel which broke out in 1948 between Russia and Yugoslavia. As soon as the Germans left in 1944, Tito and his partisan fighters set up a communist government. Although they had not needed Russian help, Tito was willing to accept Soviet advisers in Yugoslavia. He changed his mind when they made it clear they expected to interfere in Yugoslavian affairs and to lay down unfair trading arrangements. In 1948 he broke off relations with Russia, and the next year Yugoslavia was expelled from the Cominform. The west saved her from ruin by giving large quantities of aid, although Tito made no secret of his communism.

Above: bags
of flour are
loaded on to
an American
C-47 to be
flown into
west Berlin

Marshal Tito
meeting
officers of a
British
warship,
1951. After
leaving the
Cominform in
1948,
Yugoslavia
turned to
Britain and
America for
aid

Russia and Japan

In the uneasy years before World War Two, Stalin had not only to guard against the threat from Hitler but to safeguard Russia against the great military power of Japan. In 1931 the Japanese advanced from their base in Korea and occupied Manchuria. They were thus occupying lands which bordered on Russia and throughout the 1930s, there were many clashes between Russian and Japanese troops.

When Japan signed an alliance with Hitler in 1940, Stalin saw before him the frightening possibility of a war on two fronts. To prevent this, he himself signed a pact with Japan by which each country agreed that she would not attack if the other went to war. Stalin could now concentrate all his forces against Germany, while Japan began her attempt to conquer Asia with the attack on the US naval base at Pearl Harbour in December 1941.

Stalin, as early as 1943, told the Americans that he would declare war on Japan three months after the surrender of the Germans. The Red Army would need that time to transfer its force from Europe to the Eastern front in Siberia. The Americans were eager to have his help, for they reckoned the defeat of Japan would take a massive effort by the combined armies of all the allies. In return for his entry into the war, Stalin got the Americans to agree that Russia should regain the territories she had lost in the 1904–5 war.

THE WAR AGAINST JAPAN

Stalin kept his agreement. Exactly three months, to the day, after the German surrender, Russia declared war on Japan and poured troops into the Japanese occupied area of Manchuria. But by now, the Americans had less need of Russian support. Two days earlier, on 6 August, they had dropped the first atomic bomb on Hiroshima. On 14 August, after a second A-bomb had been dropped, Japan surrendered. The fighting in Manchuria went on for a few days before the Japanese armies there surrendered. Stalin announced this as a great victory and revenge for 1904–5: 'the defeat of Russian troops in 1904 left bitter memories in the mind of the people. It lay like a black spot on our country. Our people believed and hoped that a day would come when Japan would be smashed and that blot effaced. Forty years have we, the people of this old generation, waited for this day.' In fact Russia had played little part in the war. It was the atomic bomb which was much more responsible than the Red Armies for Japan's defeat.

The Cold War in Asia

Immediately Japan was defeated, disagreements between the two powers broke out. The Americans complained of the way Russia stripped Manchuria, which was China's richest industrial area, of all its heavy industrial plant. The Russians attacked the Americans for not allowing them to share in the occupation of defeated Japan. They withdrew their representative at Tokyo, complaining that the occupying Americans, under General MacArthur, treated him 'like a piece of furniture'.

Far more serious was the situation in Korea, where there was a joint occupation by American and Russian Armies. The country was divided, at the 38th parallel, into two zones and a situation developed very like that in occupied Germany. In the north the Russians set up a government dominated by Communists, some of whom were trained in Moscow. In the south the Americans held elections, but were unable to prevent bribery and force being used to produce a government which was more concerned with being anti-Communist than with restoring the country to prosperity. In 1948 the Russians withdrew their armies and the Americans followed suit the next year. Both left behind teams of specialists to train the armies of the two separate governments. The armies of the north and the south made frequent raids across the border. All of these were on the small scale until, on 25 June 1950, the North Koreans made an all-out attack on the south.

Immediately, a meeting of the United Nations Security Council was called. North Korea was declared to be the aggressor and a UN army, under the command of General Macarthur, was set up to push them back. The Americans provided most of the troops, although fourteen other nations each played a small part. It was supposed that the North Korean attack was ordered by Russia in a deliberate attempt to shift the Cold War into Asia after NATO had checked her progress in Europe. In fact it now seems more likely that the North Koreans hoped to draw Russia into the war once it had been started. All that Russia did, during the next three years, was to send enough equipment to prevent the defeat of the North Koreans. The army which eventually came to the North Korean's aid when it was being driven back through its own territory was that of a new power, Communist China.

Communist China

China had become Communist in 1949. Since the end of the Second World War there had been a civil war in China between the government forces of General Chiang Kai-shek and the Communist armies of Mao Tse-tung. The Americans had given help to Chiang, particularly in the early stages of the war, but Stalin had done very little to help the Chinese Communists. He was extremely distrustful of Communist movements that were not led from Moscow and contact between the Chinese and Russian communists had been broken in the 1930s. Knowing little of the strength of the Chinese Communists, he was startled by the ease with which they swept the Nationalists out of China to the island of Formosa. Nevertheless, he was heartened when Mao announced that China was 'leaning to one side'—the Communist side—in world affairs. In February 1950, Russia and China signed a treaty of friendship and Russia agreed to lend money and experts to build up Chinese industry. This friendship between the two vast Communist Countries with a joint population of 900 millions seemed a frightening development in the Cold War.

President Truman saw it in this way for, when the Korean war broke out, he announced that the US Seventh fleet would prevent any Chinese Communist attack on Formosa during the course of the war, appearing to suggest that Russia and China were both bent on conquests in Asia. It was not long before the Chinese and the Americans were fighting each other. In the autumn of 1950 the United Nations army had forced the North Koreans back across the 38th parallel and were pursuing them northwards towards the Chinese frontier. China sent 200,000 troops into North Korea and with these reinforcements, the United Nations troops were pushed back into South Korea.

The fighting went on until 1953, although peace negotiations began in 1951. Throughout this long period, Russia stood aside from an active part in the war, although she supplied jet fighters and other arms to the forces of North Korea.

Peace was signed not long after the death of Stalin in 1953. The war, which had looked like a spread of the Cold War from Europe, ended by leaving China as the strongest Communist power in Asia and sowed the seeds of the bitter hatred between China and America which continues today.

The UN

The United Nations action in Korea was only made possible by the fact that Russia had not been present at the meeting of the Security Council in June 1950. Her representatives had walked out six months before in protest at the UN's failure to give a seat to the new Communist government of China. China was represented in the General Assembly and the Security Council by the Nationalist government, which ruled only in Formosa. The Russians and other communist states in the UN had tried to have Communist China admitted to the UN, but their proposal was blocked by the votes of the western powers.

If the Soviet Union had attended the Security Council, they would have been able to block the United Nations action in Korea by using the veto. The veto was the special vote held by each of the five permanent members (America, Britain, France, China and Russia). If only one of these powers voted against an action upon which all the others were agreed it could not take place. Stalin had insisted on the veto in 1945 when the arrangements for the UN had been discussed at Yalta. He felt sure that the Americans would use their influence over other states, such as those in South America, to build up a block which would always out-vote the Russians. He remained suspicious of the United Nations throughout the rest of his life and the veto was used on many occasions by the Soviet Union.

11 Stalin's Last Years 1945–1953

After the War

Twenty million people died in the Great Fatherland War from disease, hunger or persecution by the Germans or Russians. The men who set off to fight or work in factories behind the Urals simply did not return. The fields were tilled by women, children and old or crippled men. There were fifty-two million women over eighteen and only thirty-one million men. Nearly every family in Russia had lost a husband, son or father. Those who remained alive were reduced to rags. Twenty-five million Russians were homeless and lived for the next few years in tents, mud huts or simple trenches dug in the ground. Seven million horses had been killed. The ground was cultivated with wooden spades or by ploughs harnessed to women and children. The countryside was reduced to grinding poverty and misery; towns were shattered ruins. There had been 1,700 towns destroyed, 31,000 factories and 84,000 schools.

All the advances made by the second revolution in the 1930s had been wiped out. Yet Stalin made the weakened, hungry, homeless Russian people begin the gigantic task of re-building. In 1946 the fourth Five Year Plan was announced. Even more than in the earlier plans, there was an emphasis on heavy industry. Electricity, iron and steel and oil production had to take priority. Home-building, clothing and food would have to wait. There was one other expensive item which was concealed from the Russian people and the world. Stalin gave secret instructions for scientists to begin work on atomic energy so that Russia could produce atomic weapons and become as strongly armed as the United States.

Once again, workers were conscripted into industry and compelled to work long hours by the fear of the labour camp. Women and children over fourteen shared in the heaviest work. The Stakhanovite campaign went on. There were new campaigns, such as one which set out to rebuild the population and replace wartime losses; a woman who had ten children was

Russia in the 'sixties: a school meal

given the title of Heroine Mother.

Every effort was made to stamp out criticism. All Russians who returned from German prisoner of war camps, or from the armies which occupied Europe after the war, were carefully 'screened' by security men. Tens of thousands were not allowed to return home but sent to work in labour camps. In the labour camps there were ten million prisoners, from Germany and other European countries, kept behind by the Russians after the war. Some were not returned until 1955.

All the targets of the fourth and fifth Five Year Plans were achieved. Russian production in the basic industries soared and her armed strength grew. MIG jet fighters took part in the Korean war; in 1949 the first Russian atomic bomb was tested.

Agriculture

The Communist terror returned to the countryside. During the war many collectives had been broken up by the peasants and, even where they had been kept in being, peasants were spending most of their time on their small garden plots and neglecting their lowly paid labour in the fields. Despite the lessons of the 1930s, collectivization was once again forced upon Russia and the new lands in the Baltic States.

Yet, the second collectivization produced no better results than the first. The average harvest for the early 1950s was still several million tons lower than it had been in 1913 and there were fewer cattle than before the First World War. The peasants were blamed for being unwilling to accept new ideas and new farming methods. Nikita Khrushchev made the suggestion that the peasants would be better disciplined if several villages were joined together to make a single collective. Then, instead of working in small teams with neighbours from their own village, they would work in large brigades of specialist farmers. In other words the peasant would become more like a factory worker, travelling to do a simple task which was laid down for him by the manager.

So the collectives were enlarged to join several villages together. Their numbers fell from 254,000 to 85,000. Yet, at the end of Stalin's life, production had still not increased. To have done any better, he would have had to transfer men and equipment from making industrial goods to producing fertilizers and farm machinery. In 1950, Russia had only one-fifth the number of tractors there were in the United States. Once Stalin had decided to catch up other nations in industrial and military strength there was little hope of improving Russian agriculture.

Political Life, 1945–53

Every aspect of Russian life was firmly controlled by Stalin in his last years. Even the Communist Party was allowed little freedom. The Central Committee was called on rare occasions and the Congress of delegates from all over the Soviet Union did not meet between 1939 and 1952. Decisions were taken in Stalin's private office; even his colleagues in the Politbureau were often not consulted.

The secret police, headed by Beria, was active in carrying out Stalin's orders. There were several purges of the Party, when many men and women who had joined during the war were expelled. The people of the minority nations were suspected of wanting to break away from the Soviet Union and three-quarters of a million people from south and west Russia were rounded up and taken to Siberia. The persecution of the Jews became as severe as under the Tsars. Jewish papers were banned and Jews expelled from positions in the government and the party.

Stalin copied the repressive methods of Tsarist Russia in another respect when he encouraged the Zhdanov campaign. Zhdanov was secretary of the Leningrad party and in the early years after the war, the man who seemed most likely to succeed Stalin. In 1946 he began a campaign to make all Soviet writers, painters and musicians, as well as scientists and historians, follow exactly the lines laid down by the Party. Writers who wrote poetry which was concerned with love or

Zhdanov

Russia in the 'sixties: new housing

any kind of personal feeling were accused of 'bourgeois think-ing' and disloyalty to Communism. All artists were expected to produce works of 'Socialist realism', which meant that paint-ings, stories and songs had to be made round subjects like the struggle to build up Russia's industry or the need to put duty to the Communist Party before personal feelings. Many writers had their work withdrawn by the censors because it did not please Zhdanov.

He also interfered in the work of scientists. All biologists were forced to agree with the scientist, Lysenko, who claimed that cells which acquired certain characteristics during their life-time would pass these on when they reproduced. In this way you could alter the process of evolution, not by careful breed-ing but through the training of animals or plants during their life-time. This was thought to be a good communist or Marxist theory because it carried the suggestion that humans could be altered by providing the right sort of society. Scientists whose experiments led them to believe that this was untrue were dis-missed or forced to admit they were mistaken. Since Stalin's death they no longer have to accept Lysenko's beliefs.

The historians' special task was to prove that nearly every important invention was the work of a Russian. Some became extremely good at this, 'finding' Russians who had invented the steam-engine and radio, and even one who had been Admiral Nelson's nurse. They also turned their hand to re-writing the life of Stalin. This task was closely supervised by

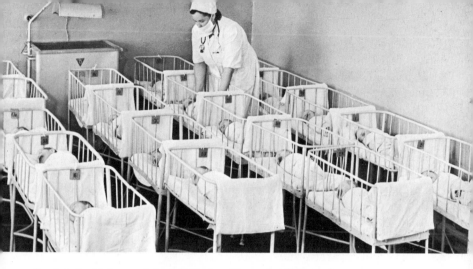

Russia in the 'sixties: newly born babies in a Siberian hospital

Stalin himself. He gloried in the sort of praise that appeared in his biography:

'Stalin is the brilliant leader and teacher of the Party, the great strategist of the Socialist Revolution, military commander and guide of the Soviet state. . . . With the name of Stalin in their hearts, the collective farmers toiled devotedly in the fields to supply the Red Army and the cities with food, and industry with raw materials. Stalin's name is cherished by the boys and girls of the Socialist land.'

In the last years of his life the flood of praise of Stalin flowed unceasingly. So many seventieth birthday greetings poured into the offices of *Pravda* that it took nearly three years before they were all printed, a few each day. His portrait hung in every office and shop and most schools. Every town had its stone or bronze statue. Many towns were named after him: Stalingrad, Stalino, Stalinsk, Stalinabad, Stalinogorsk.

But this man, who was portrayed as the guide and friend of the Russian people, had no first-hand knowledge of the country and never visited one of the collective farms he had forced upon the people. It was only on rare occasions that he left the Kremlin. A man so isolated was bound to grow suspicious of his colleagues and wonder whether they were plotting against him. Khrushchev described the Stalin of this time: 'Stalin was a very distrustful man, sickly suspicious; we knew this from our work with him. He could look at a man and say: "Why are your eyes so shifty today?", or "Why are you turning so much

137

today and avoiding looking me directly in the eyes?"'

At the end of 1952 another bloody purge seemed about to be launched. Nine doctors were suddenly arrested and accused of plotting the murder of Party leaders, including Zhdanov who had died suddenly in 1948. The charges were obviously false, like those which had followed the murder of Kirov in 1934. 'If you do not obtain confessions from them', Stalin told the Minister of Security, 'I will shorten you by a head.' Confessions were obtained—two of the nine doctors are thought to have

Russia in the 'sixties: weighing a baby in a Soviet clinic

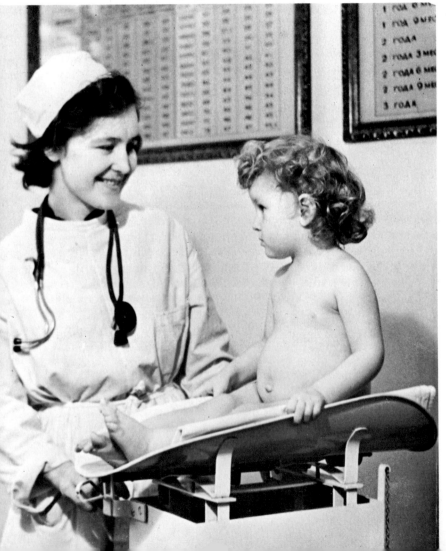

died under torture—and it was announced that the 'murders' were part of an international Jewish plot, a clear sign of Stalin's disordered mind. Would the next step be a trial of leading members of the Politbureau like the great trials of the 'thirties? The answer will never be fully known for, on 5 March 1953, Stalin died.

How great a man was Stalin? He was undeniably a cruel, ruthless man who failed to see that the true greatness of the Russians lay in their warmth and friendliness, in their love of social life, and their great music, poetry and stories. He left behind a country paralysed by fear, dullness and suspicion. One excuse for this would be that he forced the Russians to do in a lifetime what had taken two hundred years of misery and oppression in England; under Stalin they moved forward from the age of the wooden plough to that of the atomic stock-pile. On the other hand, nothing can ever excuse unnecessary cruelty, nor does it produce the best results. There were many Russians who would have made a great contribution to the country's modernization if they had been allowed to work freely—or to stay alive! Some dictatorship and certainly much hardship was probably necessary if Russia was to develop as fast as she did, but Stalin's rule was not only one of strong government but of fear, suspicion, terror and mass murder.

12 Khrushchev's Russia

Khrushchev in 1956

Collective Leadership

The day after Stalin's death, Georgi Malenkov was given Stalin's two posts of Prime Minister and Party Secretary. But his colleagues were not prepared to allow him to hold all Stalin's power and within a week he had been forced to hand over the Party secretaryship to Nikita Khrushchev. These two men were said to be part of the 'collective leadership' of Communists, who governed the Soviet Union for the next two years.

The collective leadership began to relax Stalin's terrorist system. The secret police was cut down and its heavy arms taken away. Tens of thousands of political prisoners were 'rehabilitated'; their imprisonment was said to have been unjust and they were freed. Millions of people in forced labour camps were allowed home. The new leaders encouraged a new freedom for Soviet writers. This was known as the thaw, after a novel by Ilya Ehrenberg. *The Thaw* describes a factory manager whose life is confused by private problems and by struggles to keep his job from falling into the hands of ambitious rivals. Writing like this, which suggested that factory managers and other Communist officials had human faults, had not been known in Russia for twenty years.

Ordinary men and women were more cheered by Malenkov's announcement of a New Course for the country's economic affairs. For twenty-five years, plans had put the stress on heavy industry; now Malenkov promised that the Soviet Union would expand light industry and food production at the same rate.

The new freedom spread to eastern Europe too. Senior members of the collective leadership met the Party rulers of the satellite countries to tell them that they must soften their rule. Here, in eastern Europe too, there was a wave of rehabilitation. The investigation into the trials and executions revealed horrible stories of injustices.

Many of the groups who had been powerful under Stalin feared that their influence would be weakened by the New Course. Army leaders worried about the effects on arms production if too much money was spent on food and consumer goods. Many older party members asked how long the Communist Party could keep the respect of the Soviet people without the stern controls of Stalin's day. Local party leaders could not understand a world in which they were not reporting on people, driving them to produce more industrial goods or taking grain crops away by the lorry load.

The rise of Khrushchev

These fears and anxieties gave Nikita Khrushchev his chance to rise to supreme power in the Soviet Union. His father was a poor peasant who had given up the struggle to earn a living from the land and moved to a nearby coalfield. Here Nikita, who had attended school for only three winters, went to work as an engine fitter. He was twenty-one in 1917. Previously he had showed no interest in politics, but now he joined a Bolshevik Revolutionary Committee and fought with Red Guard units against the Whites.

In 1921 he returned to the coalfield as a party official with the task of driving the workers to rebuild their shattered industry. He was successful at this and the Party sent him for four years' training in economics and communist theory. After this his rise was rapid. He became Party Secretary of a large rural district where he drove about energetically by pony-cart and sledge, bullying and persuading peasants to grow more food. He began to speak up at Party meetings in support of Stalin and to make bitter attacks on Stalin's enemies. This earned him further promotion and in 1931 he was moved to Moscow. Four years later he was Secretary of the Moscow City Communist Party, and took a leading part in purging anti-Stalinists at the time of the Great Purge. His reward was a place in the Politbureau and the Party Secretaryship of the Ukraine, Russia's largest region.

He remained in the Ukraine until 1949, although during the war, when his region was occupied by Germans, he worked in the army. In 1949 he was recalled to Moscow and was thus at the centre of power in the last years of Stalin's life. Along with Malenkov and Beria he was recognized as one of the three leading figures in the government and in the Communist Party.

After the collective leadership was set up Khrushchev

Beria

A *Pravda* picture taken in a government store after the collective leadership reduced prices

began to build a strong body of supporters who were opposed to Malenkov. He gave them an example by himself attacking Malenkov's food policy. The promise of more food would never be met, he argued, unless there was a massive campaign to build up agriculture. He launched the scheme to grow wheat in the Virgin Lands. This was an area of semi-dry soils in south-west Siberia which had never been cultivated. Khrushchev's scheme involved sowing an acreage as large as Canada's wheat fields, using 120,000 tractors. The work was done by volunteers from Komsomol, the Young Communist organisa-tion. It called on the same pioneering spirit which had built up Russian industry under Stalin.

By February 1955 Khrushchev had enough supporters to succeed in having Malenkov dismissed. The new Prime Minister was Nikolai Bulganin, but the real power now lay in Khrushchev's hands.

It soon became clear that he really had no quarrel with Malenkov's goal of giving the Soviet people a richer and fuller life. What he distrusted were Malenkov's methods, which might weaken the Communist Party. On the other hand Khrushchev had no intention of giving in to those who favoured a return to the repressive system of Stalin.

The Secret Speech

Khrushchev selected the twentieth Congress of the Soviet Communist Party as the stage for this delicate task of pushing the Soviet Union towards new policies without destroying the prestige of its Communist Party. The meeting of February 1956 was the first Party congress since Stalin died. Men and women were chosen to attend from party organisations throughout the U.S.S.R.

In the early days of the Congress Krushchev put many bold proposals before them. He argued that peaceful co-existence with the capitalist world was possible and that Russia could produce the consumer goods desired by her people. In other words the policies of the Collective Leadership and Malenkov were to go on. But these discussions were followed by a session, from which the press were kept out, at which Krush-chev made his famous 'Secret Speech'.

Nearly all of it was an attack on Stalin. Krushchev read out

The Virgin Lands scheme. Volunteer
workers taking a soil sample

Lenin's will which had criticised Stalin in 1924. For the first
time details of the purges were given and Krushchev blamed
Stalin for having a hand in the murder of Kirov which
started them. He told the delegates that Stalin had planned
military campaigns on a globe, that he was responsible for
the break with Yugoslavia and that he closed his eyes to the
true facts about agriculture.

The speech was never published in Russia but it was read
to meetings of party members. Many suffered deep shock at
this savage attack on the man whom they had grown up to
worship as the hero of all Russia's struggles.

Yet Khrushchev had been very careful to proclaim that
the Communist Party would remain in control in the Soviet
Union. Communists had to face the facts of Stalin's tyranny
but there was still the tradition of Lenin and forty years of
social and industrial progress to build on. After the initial
shock, most of the Soviet Communist Party felt gratitude to
Khrushchev for showing them the way forward.

Eastern Europe

It was a very different story in eastern Europe. There Stalinism represented Russian control over people of different
nations. When the secret speech leaked out it was taken to
herald a drastic change in the way that Russia and the
People's Democracies were bound together. Khrushchev

himself had visited Yugoslavia in 1955 and apologised to President Tito for his past treatment at the hands of Russia. In the summer of 1956 Tito visited Moscow where the Communist Parties of Yugoslavia and the Soviet Union signed a statement agreeing that countries could follow 'different roads to socialism.' In other words, Khrushchev no longer expected other Communist states to follow a master plan laid down by the Soviet Union.

This new policy and the secret speech sparked off demands for less harsh government and less control by Russia especially in Hungary and Poland. The Russians had already sacked some of the toughest Stalinists in Poland when workers' riots in June 1956 led to calls for a higher standard of living and more freedom from Russia. The Polish Communist Party appointed a new Secretary, Wadislaw Gomulka who had been imprisoned by Stalin. Gomulka was a dedicated communist but known to favour more freedom from Russian control. Khrushchev flew to Warsaw to demand that Gomulka be replaced by someone acceptable to the Russians. The Poles refused. Khrushchev, seeing that the Polish nation was behind Gomulka, gave in.

Events went much further in Hungary. In October 1956 the people of the capital, Budapest, revolted and forced leading members of the hated Communist government to flee. Communist secret policemen were hunted down and hanged. There were widespread demands for a complete break from Communism. Imre Nagy, who became Prime Minister when other leaders fled, bowed before the storm and promised elections in which the Communist Party would stand against other parties. He announced that Hungary would break her defence arrangements with the Soviet Union. This was too much for Khrushchev, already under severe attack for his softness towards Poland. Russian tanks rolled into Budapest and crushed the revolt after a few days of bloody fighting. 180,000 Hungarians fled to the west. Imre Nagy was arrested by the Russians and shot a few months later.

The ruthlessness that Khrushchev showed in Hungary prevented the break-up of the Soviet bloc. It also quietened his enemies in Russia who had argued that it was his campaign against Stalinism which had led to the situation going out of

Hungarian revolutionaries arrest a member of the Communist political police

control. Many times he made it clear that he would be ruthless again. At a meeting of authors at his own home he reminded them that Hungarian writers had been among the leading trouble makers. If Russian authors behaved in the same way he would have them shot. 'My hand would not tremble', he said.

Yet in 1957 he proved that he was in a strong enough personal position not to need to shoot his opponents. A group of Stalinists got together with Malenkov to overthrow Khrushchev. He returned from a visit to Finland to be told by the Party Praesidium that he was dismissed. Khrushchev demanded a meeting of the Central Committee of the Communist Party. The Central Committee was considered the ruling body of the Party in Lenin's day but Stalin had never consulted it.

Now its members were flown in to Moscow from all over Russia, many in military 'planes supplied by Marshall Zhukhov who was Minister of Defence and a supporter of Khrushchev. About half the people who turned up had been given their party jobs by Khrushchev. They backed him at a crowded meeting. The outcome was that it was not Khrushchev who lost his post but his enemies.

Industry and Agriculture
One of Khrushchev's chief schemes for making sure that the Communist Party kept control of Russian life was the decentralisation of industrial planning. In 1957 sixty Moscow Ministries were abolished and local Economic Councils set up

to manage industry and agriculture in more than a hundred regions. Later the number was reduced to nineteen. These Economic Councils were set up chiefly to give local Communist Party leaders a closer say in the management of Russian industry.

Khrushchev aimed in this way to give the Communist Party the credit for creating a richer life for the Russian people. He once said:

'We must help people to eat well, dress well and live well. You cannot put theory into your soup or Marxism into your clothes. If, after forty years of Communism, a person cannot have a glass of milk or a pair of shoes, he will not believe that Communism is a good thing, no matter what you tell him.'

In 1958 he dropped the sixth Five Year Plan which was only half completed and announced a new Seven Year Plan. This outlined the steps by which he hoped to improve the lives of ordinary men and women. By 1965, incomes were to rise by forty percent and there was to be a forty hour week. But the improvements were still to come about from emphasising heavy industry. Plans were laid down for a giant chemical industry which would produce vast quantities of fertilisers for the fields, artificial fibres for clothes and plastic goods for the home. Housing factories were to produce the prefabricated sections for fifteen million new flats.

The schemes came nowhere near success. One of Khrushchev's greatest weaknesses was his love of big simple ideas. Just as the chemical industry was expected to transform Russian industrial production so growing maize was Khrushchev's answer to the food shortages. More meat was urgently needed. "What kind of Communism is it that has no sausage?" Khrushchev asked. But raising more cattle for meat means growing more fodder. Maize was recommended to collective farms throughout the Soviet Union and eastern Europe. This enthusiasm had harmful results because party leaders encouraged farmers to grow it in unsuitable areas. In the end Khrushchev lost the support of the Russian peasants. They had welcomed his early measures especially when he freed the collective farms from control by the Motor Transport Stations and allowed them to buy their own machinery. By 1963 most were completely disgruntled with the low prices that the state gave for their produce and with the interference of Party officials in farm management.

Khrushchev and the World

Stalin had died leaving the Soviet Union in a state of deadlock with the west. From the west it looked as if Russian ambitions to spread Communism had been checked by the creation of NATO in 1949 and by the United Nations action in Korea. The Russian leaders felt that their country was in a weak position. Their huge armies were out-measured by the US airforce with its long range heavy bombers carrying nuclear payloads. The USA also had the economic strength to win friendship by giving aid to other nations.

Yet Russia was fast catching up with the USA as a military power. In 1949 she had exploded her first atomic weapon, four years after the Americans. In 1953 the first Soviet hydrogen bomb was tested, in the same year as the USA. Khrushchev hoped that Russia would soon be in a position to match the United States as a large-scale centre of world trade.

These were the facts behind his policy of peaceful co-existence; which laid down that there was room in the world for two super-powers to live side by side.

At Geneva, in the summer of 1955 Khrushchev attended a summit meeting. It was the first time that a Soviet leader had talked to British and United States' leaders since the war. The Soviet Union announced her willingness to end the occupation of Austria and sign a peace treaty with her.

Later in the year Khrushchev visited India and Burma. Stalin had always taken the view that Russia would not deal with non-Communists such as Pandit Nehru, India's prime minister. Khrushchev was prepared to talk to non-Communists and ready to match the USA in giving aid.

This was the start of a new Soviet policy and a new balance in world affairs. The under-developed countries could buy Soviet goods or take Soviet aid and play the two sides in the Cold War off against each other. The Soviet Union gained influence in areas where she previously had no foothold. The Middle East was an example. In 1955 Khrushchev made a deal with Egypt to supply her with arms. The USA and Britain tried to put pressure on Egypt to break away from her

Soviet connection by refusing to lend her money for the Aswan dam. The result was a great propaganda victory for Russia who did lend the money.

In 1960 the Russians came to the aid of the one-year old Cuban revolutionary government. Cuba was sold arms and her economy was propped up by an agreement to buy sugar which the USA refused to purchase after Castro's nationalisation of American property.

After he had made it clear, in 1955 and 1956, that Russia aimed to play the part of a super-power with world wide influence, Khrushchev worked to bring about a major settlement with the USA. He pointed out the dangers of nuclear rivalry: 'if the other countries fight among themselves they can be separated but if war breaks out between America and our country no-one will be able to stop it. It will be a catastrophe on a grand scale.' An agreement with America would also mean that Khrushchev went down in history as the leader who made the Soviet Union strong enough to talk on equal terms with the USA.

In 1957 the USSR launched Sputnik 1, the world's first space craft. She could then hold the lead in space exploration for several years. It could be argued that here was proof that Soviet industry and education were more successful than that of the capitalist west.

The Soviet Union and China

Throughout 1958 and 1959 the Chinese Communists watched Khrushchev with increasing sourness. Before that time they had supported him in his struggles against the Stalinists in the Soviet Union. The moment of greatest warmth between the two Communist Parties came in 1957 when Khrushchev visited China and signed agreements for aid and for sharing nuclear secrets.

But by 1959 the Chinese were angry. Khrushchev, they complained, was trying to reach an agreement with the Americans which would leave the Chinese without the protection of the Soviet Union against US attack. As Khrushchev grew more hopeful about settling international disputes without war, Mao made bitter attacks on the American 'paper tiger' and boasted that 'the east wind will prevail over the west wind', in an effort to keep the Cold War going. He was angry when Russia would not support the Chinese claim for part of Indian territory in 1959. In the same year Khrushchev ended the agreement to share nuclear secrets with China.

Communist China's tenth anniversary fell on 1 October 1959. In September, Khrushchev visited the United States. He spoke bluntly, perhaps to please Russians who distrusted America: 'I have not come to plead with you. We are no less strong than you.' Nevertheless, he succeeded in his great aim of persuading President Eisenhower to come to a summit conference in Paris in the spring of 1960. He flew back in triumph to Moscow and immediately took another 'plane to Peking for the anniversary celebrations. There he argued that war must be avoided at all costs. Yet he could not convince the Chinese.

In May 1960, the Chinese seemed to have been proved right. Just two weeks before the summit meeting was due to take place a Soviet anti-aircraft unit brought down an American U2 'plane which was flying more than 1,000 miles inside the Russian borders photographing military installations. Khrushchev demanded an apology from Eisenhower. All he got was a promise that future U2 flights would be cancelled. Khrushchev angrily refused to go on with the summit meeting.

But despite the lesser chance of agreement with America, Khrushchev chose the second half of 1960 as the time to make a final break with Mao Tse-tung. At two meetings of Communist Parties from all the world, one in Romania and one in Moscow, he attacked China and Mao himself. Khrushchev had split the world Communist movement into two. From that

Yuri Gagarin, a few moments before his first journey into space

Americans demonstrating against Khrushchev's visit to the USA, 1959

year onwards some twenty of the sixty-five or so Communist Parties in the world supported China. Khrushchev withdrew the Soviet technicians and advisers who had been working in China.

He went on to bully the USA still hoping for agreement. In 1961 he ordered the building of the Berlin Wall to stop the flood of refugees to the west. In 1962 he made an arrangement with the Cuban president, Fidel Castro, whereby Soviet missile bases would be placed on Cuban soil. Their presence was discovered by U2s before they had been equipped with missiles. President Kennedy ordered that all Russian ships bound for Cuba would be stopped until the bases were dismantled. For days the world seemed to be on the brink of a world war and then Khrushchev backed down.

No-one quite knows why Khrushchev took the great risk of challenging the US over the missile bases. Perhaps he was under pressure from Soviet leaders, perhaps he hoped to force the United States President, John F. Kennedy, to agree to a new summit conference. After his withdrawal he did not slacken in his search for agreements with the USA. The hot line telephone link was opened to make it possible for the Russian and American leaders to speak directly to each other. In 1963 the USA, Great Britain and the Soviet Union signed a treaty banning any kind of nuclear testing. Khrushchev must have known that the Chinese were well on with nuclear arms research which led to their first test explosion in October 1964.

Khrushchev's Fall

No-one can stay in power in the Soviet Union, or any other state, without building up a circle of enemies. Many Communists distrusted Khrushchev's approach to industry and agriculture and accused him of putting one 'hare-brained' scheme after another forward to catch the lime-light.

His enemies could point to the failure of the Virgin Lands scheme. Year after year the amount of crops produced fell. It was the same story in the rest of agriculture. There was a bad harvest in 1963 and the total grain crop was 27 million tons lower than in 1958.

Behind all these worries there was a great fear that Khrushchev's policies would encourage too much criticism of the

The Berlin Wall

An American Warship escorts a
Russian vessel carrying missiles
away from Cuba

Russia in the 'sixties: many Russian families can now take summer holidays away
from home at new resorts like this one in the Ukraine

Communist Party's right to rule. A second fear was that Khrushchev was risking a mighty defeat at the hands of the United States of America.

In October 1964 his colleagues on the Praesidium summoned Khrushchev back from the Black Sea where he was on holiday. They told him that he was dismissed. As in 1957, he demanded a meeting of the Central Committee. This met but refused to give Khrushchev support. After nine years his supremacy had come to an end. In those years he had opened the eyes of the Soviet people to many of their problems. He had focussed attention on agriculture and the need for consumer goods. He had taken the world a good way from the snarling hatred and distrust of the early days of the Cold War. Many of his schemes failed but his name became a symbol for a more human and less repressive Communism.

13 The Soviet Union Today

After Mr. Khrushchev's dismissal, Mr. Brezhnev became Secretary of the Communist Party and Mr. Kosygin the prime minister. They abandoned many of Khrushchev's plans which they saw as very little more than 'hare-brained schemes'. Their own measures showed how much greater are the difficulties of carrying out Khrushchev's dream of over-taking the United States.

Russia in the 'sixties: a new hotel

Agriculture

In 1965 Mr. Kosygin announced the first of a series of reforms of agriculture. Peasants were offered some of the social benefits which had been denied to them by Stalin and Khrushchev. Old age pensions and sickness payments were introduced, as well as a scheme for paying the collective farmer for his work every fortnight or month. Previously there had been no payment until the end of each year when all the profit made by the collective was shared among the members.

Under Mr. Khrushchev, party leaders were encouraged to bully farmers into giving up their private plots and the animals they kept there. Today, these tiny plots, which only average about an acre per collective farm member, produce about one-quarter of the total food supply in the USSR. Peasants market this produce themselves in the free market found in every town.

Khrushchev encouraged party officials to interfere in agriculture. The new leadership has given more freedom to farm directors to plan the most suitable activities for their collective.

Behind the question of food production lies a grave social problem of the future of village life. At the beginning of the century eight of every ten Russians lived and worked in a village; today the peasant population is just over four-tenths. The men who built the towns and factories of each Five Year Plan mostly came from rural Russia. The movement still goes on. Boys and some girls who go away to high school and college are reluctant to return to work in the villages. Young men try hard to find a city job after they have completed their three years of military service.

One very sad aspect of rural life is the great proportion of lonely women. These are the sisters and widows of the nine million peasants killed in the war, as well as those younger women whose menfolk have left for a new life in the towns. The movement from the countryside goes on despite the many recent improvements. In the last few years sales of television sets and washing machines to peasants have gone up enormously and it is now hard to tell a peasant from a city dweller by his dress. Yet, on the other hand, rural Russia is still another, poorer, world cut off from the towns by the lack of well-made roads and even more by sharp differences in standards of living. Even a crowded city apartment may be attractive against wooden homes, half of which still have no electric light and where two-thirds of the peasant occupiers must bake their own bread.

Collective farms were enlarged in the fifties so that many now include the population of four or more villages. This helped the poorest villages to improve their standard of living but the communities are still not large enough to build up the comforts of city life. Larger collectives have also resulted in sharp differences between levels of payment. At the head of a collective farm will be its chairman who is assisted by a number of agricultural experts. Their plans will be put into operation by brigade leaders who are responsible for organising the labour in each village, or part of a village, and by section heads in charge of animal breeding, machine maintenance and so on. These administrators earn up to seven times as much as labourers, or 'horse and hand' workers. In between the administrators and the horse and hand workers come the 'mechanisers' who drive and maintain tractors, combined harvesters and electrical equipment. They may earn as much as four or five times as much as a labourer. Most of the administrators and mechanisers are men whereas the greater part of the horse and hand workers are women.

Managing Industry

Industry gave even more problems than agriculture to the men who followed Khrushchev. Ever since Stalin began the Five Year Plans there had been close control of every factory in the Soviet Union. This was probably the only way in which she could have brought about tremendous growth in heavy industry, and armed for the war against Hitler and to match United States strength in the Cold War.

Today, the USSR places greater emphasis on consumer goods and increasingly finds that the sort of planning she used in the past is neither suitable nor efficient. It is quite easy to lay down central targets for heavy industry, to demand that, for instance, a coking plant produces so many tons of fuel for the steel industry. But if the planner has to work for more motor cars or washing machines his task becomes immediately more difficult. The number of suppliers to the assembling factory, each of whom ought to have a production target, will be very much greater. It might well be that an enterprise supplying, say, splinter-proof glass will have machines lying idle if it is allowed to produce only for the motor car industry and has no freedom to develop a second line, perhaps supplying glass for shop fronts. Nor can central planning take into account new discoveries such as means of replacing an expensive metal part with a cheap plastic one.

In 1965 Mr. Kosygin scrapped the regional economic councils set up by Khrushchev. All they had done was to raise the number of planners and add some very inexperienced local men to the great number who already interfered in an industrial enterprise. He recentralised overall planning in Moscow, but went out of his way to state that managers would have much more freedom to work out their own methods of production and sales providing that they kept to the general plan laid down in Moscow. Yet today controls over banking, prices, export markets and so on, still hinder the freedom of the enterprises.

Czechoslovakia

The pressure for changes in the economic planning was stronger in the Eastern European states because central control is associated in people's minds with Russian domination over Poles, Hungarians, Germans, Romanians and Bulgarians. In the later 1960s each of these countries carried out economic reforms more far reaching than those in Russia. Their first object was to give more freedom to factory and farm managers. But other changes followed including greater freedom to trade with countries outside the Soviet bloc. In Hungary, for instance, individual managers may make their own decisions about exports and imports—provided they have the support of the State bank.

Allowing freedom in economic planning means letting certain groups of people make decisions which are not always in line with those of the Communist leadership. Eastern European leaders were faced with the problem of stopping these differences of opinion from turning into criticisms of the Communist Party or the Soviet Union. Throughout the sixties most of them tried to control political opinion, although relaxing their hold over religion. But this had not happened in Czechoslovakia.

There, in the most industrialised of the Eastern European states, rigid Communist Party control had been maintained until the end of 1967. Other states, such as Romania had made far greater progress towards economic reform, and political life in Poland and Hungary had become far less controlled. Demands for change arose from every side in Czechoslovakia; from experts who wanted a freer economic system, from students and intellectuals demanding freedom from political censorship, from workers and the great masses of the people who believed that Russian control and their own Communist Party were holding back the Czechoslovak nation.

In the spring of 1968 the Czechoslovak Communist Party turned against its secretary Mr. Novotny and replaced him with Alexander Dubcek. Mr. Dubcek very quickly encouraged steps to give 'socialism a human face'. Supporters of Novotny were dismissed and there were many rehabilitations of men who had been unjustly imprisoned or executed since Czechoslovakia became communist in 1948. Rigid control of industry was removed. More important for the future was the Action Programme of the Czechoslovak Communist Party proclaimed in April. This called for freedom of speech and in the press, and for the right to move freely inside and out of the country. Censorship of the press and television was lifted and journalists and commentators discussed the new developments. The keynote of the few months of the 'Prague Spring' was the belief that the Communist Party had no right to rule unless it could persuade the Czechoslovak people to follow its lead.

This idea, that the Party should prove its right to leadership, horrified most Moscow Communists. Although they themselves were carrying out some reforms in the economic management of the USSR they had never allowed the Party's right to rule to be questioned. However many Soviet people, particularly intellectuals, were in sympathy with the Prague Spring. Moreover, the Czechoslovak reforms were seen as a threat to Communist rule in other eastern European countries and some of their leaders were pressing the Russians to intervene.

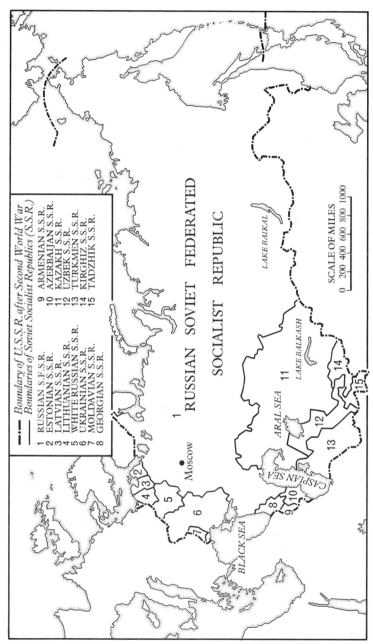

The Soviet Union

Boundary of U.S.S.R. after Second World War
Boundaries of Soviet Socialist Republics (S.S.R.)

1 RUSSIAN S.F.S.R.
2 ESTONIAN S.S.R.
3 LATVIAN S.S.R.
4 LITHUANIAN S.S.R.
5 WHITE RUSSIAN S.S.R.
6 UKRAINIAN S.S.R.
7 MOLDAVIAN S.S.R.
8 GEORGIAN S.S.R.
9 ARMENIAN S.S.R.
10 AZERBAIJAN S.S.R.
11 KAZAKH S.S.R.
12 UZBEK S.S.R.
13 TURKMEN S.S.R.
14 KIRGHIZ S.S.R.
15 TADZHIK S.S.R.

RUSSIAN SOVIET FEDERATED
SOCIALIST REPUBLIC

Moscow

LAKE BAIKAL

LAKE BALKASH

ARAL SEA

CASPIAN SEA

BLACK SEA

SCALE OF MILES
0 200 400 600 800 1000

When negotiations in August 1968 between the Czech and Soviet leaders did not stop the reforms, Soviet troops supported by forces from Bulgaria, Poland, East Germany and Hungary invaded Czecholslovakia. There was little fighting, yet the invaders found that they were opposed by every social group in the country. The army police, trade unions, all refused to co-operate. The Communist Party and the parliament both declared the Russian action to be aggression. Yet the Soviet leaders did not turn back. Dubcek, together with the Prime Minister, was arrested and flown to Moscow. They were released after negotiations but this was the start of a two year period in which nearly everything that had been built up in the spring of 1968 was undone.

The censorship of press and radio was restored. The men who had led the 1968 reform movement were dismissed from their posts in the Party or government. A young student, Jan Palach, burned himself to death in January 1969 as a protest. This action moved many Czechoslovaks to continue their resistance to the Russian pressure but it also strengthened the determination of some conservative Czechoslovak leaders to hasten the end of Dubcek and all his supporters. In April 1969 Mr. Dubcek was replaced as Secretary of the Communist Party by Gustav Husak. It is unfair to compare Mr. Husak with the Communists who ruled Czechoslovakia before 1968, yet his task has quite clearly been to wipe out all the political reforms of the Prague Spring.

The Party and the Writers

The greatest of today's Soviet writers is Alexander Solzhenitsyn. For years he was unable to have his books published in the USSR and was under attack from the Communist Party, and even fellow writers, for his criticism of the lack of liberty in the Soviet Union. He had served a long prison camp sentence under Stalin and was probably saved from another in recent times only by his world fame. In 1974, he was allowed to leave the U S S R and settle as a permanent exile in western Europe. His place as the best known critic of the Soviet regime was taken by Andrei Sakharov, a scientist who is also possibly protected by his international reputation. Others among the intellectuals, scientists and writers who make up the strongest opposition to the Soviet regime have to carry out their activity 'underground'. Journals such as the *Chronicle of Current Events* are circulated secretly with details of secret police arrests and documents of protest. Stories and articles which would never get past the censorship are published *samizdat* (which means 'self-publishing'). They are typed or mimeographed and passed around from hand to hand.

A Russian survey of 783 persons who signed protest petitions showed that 22 percent were writers or other artists, and 45 percent university research workers or teachers, while only 6 percent were ordinary workers. The mass of the Russians have not opposed the Soviet authorities in the same way that the Czech workers supported their intellectuals in 1968. This may be because ordinary Russians have never been used to political freedom as the people of Czechoslovakia were before 1948.

Town Life in the Seventies

The position of ordinary men and women in the 1970s is best not compared with living and political conditions in the rest of the world but with the state of Russian society when the Bolsheviks seized power.

In fifty years the number of town dwellers has gone up from 18 million to 150 million. More than a hundred million people live in towns or parts of towns which have been built only in the past forty years. Each year this figure increases by another three or four million.

These figures show how Russians have put behind them the village lives described in the beginning of this book and entered into a new world. Today housing supply is one of the most talked-of problems in the Soviet Union. In the early sixties a policy of providing not one room but one flat per family was announced. Khrushchev's policies in house-building were not always successful yet, by the end of the 1960s, the Soviet Union was building 9.6 housing units (flats or houses) per thousand people, while the USA achieved 7.9 and Britain 7.3. Standards are still poor. A Moscow family of three has on average only sixteen by thirteen feet of living space.

This is the reason why private housing is going ahead fast.

No-one in the Soviet Union may own private property but certain items of 'personal' property such as a motor car and one house are permitted. Richer party officials and well-paid Russians, such as writers, may build themselves a country house or 'dacha' on the edge of a city. Co-operative groups band together to share in the building of an apartment block.

The people who live in Russian towns vary greatly in their standard of living. Family incomes in the lowest paid groups can be as low as one-seventh or one-eighth of that earned by a senior Party official or a professor or a colonel. This difference is levelled out to a much greater extent than in western countries by social welfare benefits such as children's allowances. Families spend most of their income on food. Other costs, such as housing rents and transport, are very low; cinema seats and books cost only a few pence each.

Towns vary greatly. The oldest and largest is Moscow which has a population of $6\frac{1}{2}$ million. The second city, Leningrad, has about $3\frac{3}{4}$ million inhabitants. These lie in the Russian Republic which occupies nearly three-quarters of the whole area of the Soviet Union and has over half the population. One of the great developments in the Russian Republic under Communism has been the development of towns in Siberia. Most of them lie in the southern Urals but others stretch eastwards along the Trans-Siberian railway from which many new spur lines have been laid down. These new towns are copies of the urban centres of European Russia. Some of them are huge; others are little more than camps around new mining or engineering developments. Siberian towns and cities are unpopular with most Russians who would rather live in European Russia, yet they are very important. Siberia is the Soviet Union's expanding frontier and her future as a great industrial power depends on the continued opening up of this once empty region.

Other famous Soviet towns lie outside the Russian Republic but in one of the other fourteen republics of the Union.

These are the homes of the minority people absorbed by the Tsarist Empire. In the late nineteenth century many of them suffered under the persecutions which followed from the Russification of the Empire. The Communists claim that this has been ended with the establishment of the USSR which is officially a federal union. Yet, of course, the government has never allowed the national republics any serious share in major policy decisions. Some cultural variety has been encouraged. Education, at least in the earlier school years, is carried out in the language of the nation and there has been great stress preserving national costume and folk-lore and giving help to groups of national singers and dancers. The result is that the Soviet Union presents a great variety to the traveller.

Soviet Foreign Policy

The fact that the Soviet Union today emphasises such problems as housing show just how much social and economic progress she has made in the past half century. Many of her difficulties are no different from those experienced by the western nations. Her foreign policy, too, is more and more influenced by the fact that she is an advanced industrialised state.

A recent estimate suggests that she leads the world in stocks of nuclear weapons of heavy yield, although the USA has a greater strength in tactical nuclear weapons. At the end of the 1960s it was reckoned that the USSR possessed 380 ocean-going submarines with perhaps 80 carrying ballistic missiles. These mobile and secret launching sites play an important part in giving the Soviet Union strategic equality with the USA.

What use has the Soviet Union made of her strength since Khrushchev fell? In the middle sixties she increased her middle eastern influence particularly by her support of Egypt. The dangers of this were obvious when Israeli forces easily destroyed the Russian-armed Egyptians in the Six-Day War of 1967. Since then, although she has supplied further arms, the Soviet Union has tried to hold back Egypt. After Egypt's defeat in a further war against Israel in 1974 she expelled all the Soviet military and technical advisers in the country.

In Asia, Soviet policy in the sixties showed her anxiety about the growth of Chinese influence. In 1966 Russian leaders brought about a truce in the India-Pakistan war by calling leaders of both sides to a meeting in Tashkent. This contrasted with the action of the Chinese who tried to intervene in favour of Pakistan by threatening India's north-eastern borders. There have been bitter exchanges about the Chinese claim that the Soviet Union was giving only the most limited help to the north Vietnamese in their struggle against the USA. The USSR is as anxious as the USA to bring the Vietnam conflict to an end. Overshadowing these questions was the threat of actual conflict with the Chinese Republic along the frontier which separates the two countries. There were some 5,000 clashes in the 1960s and in 1969 a burst of severe fighting broke out along the Amur and Assuri rivers. Quite obviously, the Russians regard the growing power of China as the most serious problem for the future.

In this respect Soviet policy changed very little since the time of Mr. Khrushchev. Nor did she give up some willingness to negotiate with the USA. In 1969 Soviet and American negotiators met for the first of the Strategic Arms Limitation Talks, despite the distrust of the USA held by some Soviet leaders. Two facts probably led the Soviet government to go ahead. One was the enormous cost of Soviet armament. The other was awareness of the number of places in the world where misunderstanding of each other's policies could bring the United States and the Soviet Union into disastrous conflict. World peace rests on the hope that the leaders of the two great powers continue to recognise that they both have responsibility for solving these problems.

Glossary

Autocracy—A system of government in which all power was held by one man, the autocrat. In Russia the Tsar, or emperor, was the autocrat.

Autonomous Republic—Areas which contain people of different nationality, speaking a different language from the majority of the people in one of the Republics of the Soviet Union. They are allowed limited control over their own affairs, particularly in education.

Bolshevik—One of the two wings of the Russian Social Democratic Party. The word means 'majority man' in Russian. The name was dropped for 'Communist' after the Bolsheviks seized power.

Cadet Party—The Constitutional Democratic, or Liberal, Party, which was founded before the elections to the first Duma in 1906.

Capitalist—A man who has the funds which enable him to set up in business and make profits. A capitalist society is one where businesses are expected to make profits for their owners and shareholders. This is prohibited in Communist societies.

Cell—The lowest part of the organization of the Communist Party. Cells are formed by a small number of Party members living in the same district or working in the same work-place.

Cheka—The secret police of early Communist days.

Cominform—The Communist Information Bureau set up by the Soviet Union in 1947 to link the communist parties of eastern Europe and those in France and Italy. It was disbanded in 1961.

Comintern—The Communist International, set up by Lenin in 1919. It was intended as a rival to the Second Socialist International of non-communist labour and socialist parties.

Control Commission—A Communist Party organization responsible for investigating complaints against party members. It soon became the body which sought out and purged disloyal members.

Duma—The parliament set up after the 1905 revolution. It never had as many powers as an English parliament. Four Dumas were elected 1905–17.

Gosplan—The organization which planned and controlled Russian industry and agriculture under Stalin's five year plans.

Holy Synod—The committee of Bishops which advised the Tsar on the affairs of the Russian Orthodox Church. Its chairman, the Procurator of the Holy Synod, was not a priest but one of the Tsar's most important ministers.

Intellectual—To Lenin, a revolutionary intellectual, was a man who understood the theories of Marx and could take the lead in persuading workers and peasants to follow the Communists.

International, or Socialist International—Joint organizations of socialist parties and groups from different countries. The First International was founded by Karl Marx. The Second International was set up in 1889 and still exists. The Third International, or Comintern, was closed in World War Two. Trotsky founded a Fourth International of revolutionary communists.

Kulak—A rich peasant.

Liberalism—'Liberal' and 'Liberalism' come from the Latin word for 'free'. A nineteenth-century liberal believed in setting people free from close control by autocratic governments, and in replacing them by parliamentary governments. Most liberals were not in favour of socialist ideas about making all men equal in rights and wealth.

Menshevik—The non-revolutionary wing of the Russian Social Democratic Party. Most Mensheviks were working men and members of trade unions.

Narodnik—Russian for 'man of the people'. Narodniks believed that Russia would become great if the peasants could be awakened out of their ignorance and superstition, and if they had more freedom.

NEP—New Economic Policy. A return to private trading in the last years of Lenin's life.

Octobrist—A group of Russian politicians who wanted very few changes in Russian life and were determined to keep the Duma in being.

OGPU—Sometimes known as the GPU. The political police under Stalin.

Okhrana—The secret police of Tsarist days.

Orthodox Church—The Russian Orthodox Church had split away from the Greek or Byzantine Orthodox Church in the sixteenth century. Thus it practised a different form of worship from the Latin or Roman Catholic Church. It was the Orthodox Church which had brought the cyrillic alphabet to Russia.

Politbureau—The political bureau (or committee) of the Communist Party. The dozen or so men who lead the Party.

Social Democrat—Before 1917 Social Democrats were Marxist socialists of both the left and the right; those who believed in overthrowing the capitalist state by revolution and those who accepted capitalism but fought for workers' rights. After the revolution the socialist movement has been split into Communists and Social Democrats. In many countries the Labour Party is known as the Social Democratic Party.

Social Revolutionary—The SRs worked for a peasants' revolution which would lead to the confiscation of the nobles' land. Most of its leaders were, however, educated men. They also were responsible for the terrorist attacks on the Tsar and his officials.

Soviet—Russian word meaning 'council'. In theory the Soviet Union is governed by soviets elected by the people.

Tsar—Sometimes Czar. The emperor of Russia. An empress ruling in her own right is a *Tsaritsa*. The wife of a Tsar is a *Tsarina*.

White—An opponent of a Communist or 'Red' government.

Zemstvo—Councils set up in 1864 to provide services for local districts. The correct Russian plural is *zemstva*.

Further Reading

Written for school libraries

A. CASH, *The Russian Revolution* (Jackdaw no 42) Cape.

J. CHARNOCK, *Russia, the Land and the People*, Bodley Head, 1960.

A. EARL, *The Story of Russia*, ULP, 1967.

J. HASLER, *The Making of Russia*, Longman, 1969.

D. HEATER, *The Cold War*, OUP, 1965.

J. KENNET, *The Growth of Modern Russia*, Blackie, 1967.

A. KETTLE, *Marx*, Weidenfeld and Nicholson, 1963.

D. MACK, *Lenin and the Russian Revolution* (Then and There Series).

S. PICKERING, *Twentieth-Century Russia*, 1965 OUP.

E. M. ROBERTS, *Lenin and the downfall of Tsarist Russia*, Methuen, 1966.

—*Stalin: Man of Steel*, Methuen, 1968.

J. ROBOTTOM (ed) *Making the Modern World: Russia*, Longman, 1972.

WRIGHT MILLER, *The Young Traveller in Russia*, Phoenix, 1958.

—*Russians as People*, Phoenix, 1960.

Other Books ·

I. DEUTSCHER, *Stalin*, Pelican, 1966.

M. FRANKLAND, *Khrushchev*, Pelican, 1966.

C. HILL, *Lenin and the Russian Revolution*, Pelican, 1971.

J. MILLER, *Life in Russia Today*, Batsford, 1969.

D. SCHUB, *Lenin*, Pelican, 1966.

A. WERTH, *Russia: Hopes and Fears*, Pelican, 1969.

Visual Aids

Lenin to Khrushchev (History of Russia Part 4) Common Ground, 1972.

Index